COUSCOUS RECIPES

Know the Culture and Recipe of Preparation

(Easy Simple Recipes Delicious Couscous Cookbook)

Shaun Wallen

Published by Alex Howard

© **Shaun Wallen**

All Rights Reserved

Couscous Recipes: Know the Culture and Recipe of Preparation (Easy Simple Recipes Delicious Couscous Cookbook)

ISBN 978-1-990169-89-2

All rights reserved. No part of this guide may be reproduced in any form without permission in writing from the publisher except in the case of brief quotations embodied in critical articles or reviews.

Legal & Disclaimer

The information contained in this book is not designed to replace or take the place of any form of medicine or professional medical advice. The information in this book has been provided for educational and entertainment purposes only.

The information contained in this book has been compiled from sources deemed reliable, and it is accurate to the best of the Author's knowledge; however, the Author cannot guarantee its accuracy and validity and cannot be held liable for any errors or omissions. Changes are periodically made to this book. You must consult your doctor or get professional medical advice before using any of the suggested remedies, techniques, or information in this book.

Table of contents

Part 1 1
Chapter 1: Easy Couscous Recipes 2
Couscous I 2
(Tagine) 2
(Moroccan Style I) 2
Couscous Ii 4
(Savory, Almonds, And Tomatoes) 4
Couscous Iii 6
(Sun Dried Tomatoes, Olives, Feta, And Garbanzos) 6
(Greek Style) 6
Couscous Iv 9
(Quinoa, Onions, And Farro) 9
Couscous V 11
(Garlic, Corn, Black Beans, Lime, And Jalapenos) 11
(Mexican Style) 11
Couscous Vi 13
(Almonds, Raisins, And Lemon) 13
(Moroccan Style Ii) 13
Couscous Vii 15
(Jalapenos, Peas, And Mint) 15
Couscous Viii 17
(Chicken, Cucumbers, And Parsley) 17
Couscous Ix 19
(Lime And Chicken) 19
Couscous X 21

(Peppers, Corn, And Black Beans) 21
Couscous Xi 23
(Creamy Parsley, Chickpeas, And Almonds) 23
Couscous Xii 25
(Veggie Turkey Couscous Bits) 25
Couscous Xiii 27
(Squash And Garbanzos) 27
(Moroccan Style Iii) 27
Couscous Xiv 29
(Cherry Tomatoes, Onions, And Basil) 29
Couscous Xv 31
(Mangos, And Salsa) 31
Couscous Xvi 33
(Moroccan Salmon Cake) 33
Couscous Xvii 36
(Feta, Balsamic, And Asparagus) 36
Couscous Xviii 38
(Peppers, Cucumbers, And Olives) 38
(Greek Style Ii) 38
Couscous Xix 40
(Cloves, Onions, Tomatoes, And Chicken) 40
(Moroccan Style Iv) 40
Couscous Xx 42
(Almonds, Cilantro, And Curry) 42
Couscous Xxi 44
(Spicy Chicken And Carrots) 44
Couscous Xxii 46

(Peppers, Shrimp, And Feta) 46
Couscous Xxiii 48
(Pepper, Lemon, And Cilantro) 48
Couscous Xxiv 50
(Lemons, Parsley, Basil, Lettuce) 50
Couscous Xxv 52
(Creamy Mushrooms And Pork) 52
Couscous Xxvi 54
(Breakfast I) 54
Couscous Xxvii 56
(Apricots, Raisins, Almonds, And Dates) 56
(Moroccan Style V) 56
Couscous Xxviii 58
(Garlic, Roma Tomatoes, And Monterey) 58
Couscous Xxviii 60
(Tomatoes, Mozzarella, Basil, And Mint) 60
Couscous Xxx 62
(Almonds, Ham, Ginger, And Broccoli) 62
Couscous Xxxi 64
(Feta, Cucumbers, Jalapenos, Basil, And Cilantro) 64
Couscous Xxxii 66
(Peppers, Garlic, Onions, Mushrooms, And Dates) 66
Couscous Xxxiii 68
(Cucumbers, Capers, And Dates) 68
Couscous Xxxiv 70
(Kebabs) 70
(Moroccan Style Vi 70

Couscous Xxxv 72

(Carrots, Harissa, Peppers, Chicken, And Sausage) 72

Couscous Xxxvi 75

(Garlic, Kale, And Parmesan) 75

Couscous Xxxvii 77

(Savory, Parsley, Lemon, And Tomatoes) 77

Couscous Xxxviii 79

(Buttery Chives And Cheddar) 79

Couscous Xxxix 81

(Tomatoes And Tarragon) 81

Couscous Xl 83

(Pine Nuts, Currants, And Pork) 83

Couscous Xli 86

(Bacon, Balsamic, And Curry) 86

Couscous Xlii 88

(Pecans, Parmesan, And Pesto) 88

Couscous Xliii 91

(Honey Rutabaga) 91

Couscous Xliv 93

(Green Beans And Black Beans) 93

Couscous Xlv 95

(Tabbouleh I) 95

Couscous Xlvi 97

(Scallops, Parsley, And Parmesan) 97

Couscous Xlvii 99

(Lentils, Onions, Feta, And Cranberries) 99

Couscous Xlviii 101

(Pine Nuts And Oranges) 101
Couscous Xlix 103
(Buttery Rosemary) 103
Couscous L 105
(Mexican Pineapple And Beans) 105
Couscous Li 107
(Crab, Clams, Bok Choy, And Tomatoes) 107
Couscous Lii 109
(Saffron And Harissa) 109
(Persian Style) 109
Part 2 111
Introduction 112
1. Mouth-Watering Mayan Couscous 112
2. One Of A Kind Savory Couscous 114
3. Delectable Spiced Couscous 115
4. Fragrant Couscous Royale 117
5. Luscious Spinach & Onion Couscous 119
6. Incredible Spontaneous Couscous 120
7. Devil May Care Couscous Primavera 121
8. Awesome Kittencal's Greek Couscous 123
9. Dynamic Curried Couscous 125
10. Snappy Cauliflower Couscous 126
11. Stimulating Cranberry Couscous Salad 127
12. Tasty Mediterranean Couscous Salad 128
13. Tempting Black Bean & Couscous Salad 129
14. Wholesome Spicy Vegetable Couscous 131
15. Relishing Red Bell Pepper Couscous 133

16. Rich Saffron Couscous 134
17. Ambrosial Apricot Couscous 135
18. Exquisite Balsamic Chicken With Garlic Couscous 137
19. Savory Greek Couscous 138
20. Eye-Opener Moroccan Mushroom Couscous 139
21. Scrumptious Fresh Mozzarella, Tomato, & Basil Couscous Salad 141
22. Appealing Couscous Gourmet 142
23. Delectable Corn Couscous 143
24. Delicious Couscous Toss 144
25. Delish Couscous Caprice 145
26. Divine Baked Couscous With Summer Squash 147
27. Heavenly Algerian Couscous 148
28. Inviting Lemon Couscous 150
29. Tantalizing Asian-Style Couscous 151
30. Yummy Butternut Squash & Couscous 152
31. Choice Moroccan Couscous 154
32. Tasteful Mandarin Couscous Salad 156
33. Ambrosia Golden Couscous 157
34. Tempting Israeli Couscous & Cheese 158
35. Titillating Lentil & Couscous Salad 160
36. A Shocker Couscous With A Kick 161
37. Gotta Have It Jeweled Couscous 162
Pesto And Feta Couscous Fritters 164
Couscous Stuffed Tomatoes 165
Toasted Almond Israeli Couscous 166
South Of The Border Dip 167

- Couscous 'N' Cheese ... 168
- Mediterranean Salad ... 169
- Couscous Cleanse ... 170
- No Cream Broccoli Cheese Soup ... 172
- Caramelised Onion And Mushroom Quiche With Couscous Crust ... 173
- Caprese Couscous Salad ... 174
- Chicken And Zucchini Couscous Sauté ... 175
- Roasted Butternut Squash With Israeli Couscous ... 176
- Spicy Fish And Sausage Soup ... 178
- Roasted Moroccan Couscous With Eggplant ... 179
- Chicken And Mini-Dumplings ... 181
- Lemon Salmon With Green Onion Couscous ... 182
- Rhubarb Couscous Crisp ... 184
- Chocolate And Coconut Couscous Bars ... 185
- Honey Cinnamon Couscous Pudding ... 186
- Watermelon And Feta Couscous Parfait ... 187

Part 1

Chapter 1: Easy Couscous Recipes

Couscous I

(Tagine)

(Moroccan Style I)

Ingredients

- 2 tbsps olive oil
- 8 skinless, boneless chicken thighs, cut into 1-inch pieces
- 1 eggplant, cut into 1 inch cubes
- 2 large onions, thinly sliced
- 4 large carrots, thinly sliced
- 1/2 C. dried cranberries
- 1/2 C. chopped dried apricots
- 2 C. chicken broth
- 2 tbsps tomato paste
- 2 tbsps lemon juice
- 2 tbsps all-purpose flour
- 2 tsps garlic salt
- 1 1/2 tsps ground cumin
- 1 1/2 tsps ground ginger
- 1 tsp cinnamon
- 3/4 tsp ground black pepper
- 1 C. water
- 1 C. couscous

Directions

- Get a bowl, mix until smooth: black pepper, broth, cinnamon, tomato paste, ginger, flour, cumin, and garlic salt.

- Stir fry your chicken in olive oil until browned all over but still slightly uncooked.
- Now put the chicken into your crock pot along with the eggplant. Then add: apricots, onions, cranberries, and carrots.
- Add the broth mix too.
- For 5 hrs cook with the high setting.
- Now get a big pot and get your water boiling.
- Once it is boiling pour in your couscous.
- Get the mix boiling again, then place a lid on the pot and shut the heat.
- Let the couscous sit in the hot water for 7 mins. Then stir it.
- When the chicken is finished serve over the couscous.
- Enjoy.

Amount per serving (8 total)

Timing Information:

Preparation	Cooking	Total Time
30 m	5 h	5 h 30 m

Nutritional Information:

Calories	380 kcal
Fat	15.2 g
Carbohydrates	38.5g
Protein	22.3 g
Cholesterol	65 mg
Sodium	571 mg

* Percent Daily Values are based on a 2,000 calorie diet.

Couscous Ii

(Savory, Almonds, And Tomatoes)

Ingredients

- 1 C. water
- 1 tsp dried savory
- 1 tsp dried parsley
- 1 pinch crushed red pepper flakes
- 1 tbsp chicken bouillon granules
- 1/2 C. pearl (Israeli) couscous
- 1 lemon, zest grated
- 1/2 C. toasted slivered almonds
- 1/2 C. chopped celery
- 1/3 C. chopped onion
- 1/2 tomato, seeded and chopped
- 1 tbsp olive oil
- salt and black pepper to taste

Directions

- Boil the following for 2 mins: bouillon, savory, pepper flakes, and parsley.
- Now add the couscous and let it gently boil with a lower level of heat for 12 mins.
- Place a lid on the pot and shut the heat.
- Once the couscous has lost its heat remove any liquid that is left.
- Get a bowl, combine: olive oil, zest, tomato, almonds, couscous mix, onions, and celery.
- Add your preferred amount of pepper and salt and the place the contents in the fridge for at least 30 mins covered with plastic wrap.
- Enjoy.

Amount per serving (3 total)

Timing Information:

Preparation	Cooking	Total Time
20 m	10 m	1 h 30 m

Nutritional Information:

Calories	266 kcal
Fat	14.3 g
Carbohydrates	27g
Protein	7.9 g
Cholesterol	< 1 mg
Sodium	401 mg

* Percent Daily Values are based on a 2,000 calorie diet.

Couscous III

(Sun Dried Tomatoes, Olives, Feta, And Garbanzos)

(Greek Style)

Ingredients

- 1/4 C. chicken broth
- 1/2 C. water
- 1 tsp minced garlic
- 1/2 C. pearl (Israeli) couscous
- 1/4 C. chopped sun-dried tomatoes
- 1/4 C. sliced Kalamata olives
- 2 tbsps crumbled feta cheese
- 1 C. canned garbanzo beans, rinsed and drained
- 1 tsp dried oregano
- 1/2 tsp ground black pepper
- 1 tbsp white wine vinegar
- 1 1/2 tsps lemon juice

Directions

- Boil your garlic in the broth for 3 mins. Then add in your couscous.
- Place a lid on the pot and shut the heat.
- Let the couscous sit in the hot water for 7 mins and then stir it.
- Get a bowl, combine: black pepper, beans, vinegar, tomatoes, oregano, lemon juice, cheese, olives, and couscous.
- Stir the mix and serve at room temp.

- Enjoy.

Amount per serving (3 total)

Timing Information:

Preparation	Cooking	Total Time
20 m	5 m	45 m

Nutritional Information:

Calories	254 kcal
Fat	5.6 g
Carbohydrates	42.4g
Protein	9 g
Cholesterol	6 mg
Sodium	592 mg

* Percent Daily Values are based on a 2,000 calorie diet.

Couscous Iv

(Quinoa, Onions, And Farro)

Ingredients

- 6 1/2 C. water, divided
- 1 C. red quinoa
- 1 C. pearl (Israeli) couscous
- 1 C. farro
- 1 cucumber, seeded and chopped
- 1/2 red onion, chopped
- 1 orange bell pepper, seeded and chopped
- 1 yellow squash, seeded and chopped
- 1/2 C. extra-virgin olive oil
- 1 lemon, juiced
- 1/2 tsp kosher salt
- 1 (6 oz.) container crumbled feta cheese

Directions

- For 2 mins boil your quinoa in 2 C. of water. Then place a lid on the pot, set the heat to low, and the let quinoa cook for 17 mins.
- Simultaneously cook the couscous in boiling water (1.5 C.) for 12 mins in a covered pot.
- At the same time boil your farro for 26 mins in 3 C. of water, in a covered pot as well.
- Once everything is done get a bowl, combine: squash, quinoa, bell peppers, couscous, onions, cucumber and farro.
- Top with a dressing of: salt, lemon juice, and olive oil.
- Place a plastic covering over the bowl and cool it in the fridge for 1 hr.

- Before serving top the salad with some feta.
- Enjoy.

Amount per serving (8 total)

Timing Information:

Preparation	Cooking	Total Time
20 m	30 m	2 h 50 m

Nutritional Information:

Calories	424 kcal
Fat	20.9 g
Carbohydrates	50.3g
Protein	11.6 g
Cholesterol	19 mg
Sodium	370 mg

* Percent Daily Values are based on a 2,000 calorie diet.

Couscous V

(Garlic, Corn, Black Beans, Lime, And Jalapenos)

(Mexican Style)

Ingredients:

- 1 cup couscous
- 1/2 tsp ground cumin
- 1 tsp salt, or to taste
- 1 1/4 cups boiling water
- 1 clove unpeeled garlic
- 1 (15 oz.) can black beans, rinsed and drained
- 1 cup canned whole kernel corn, drained
- 1/2 cup finely chopped red onion
- 1/4 cup chopped fresh cilantro
- 1 jalapeno pepper, minced
- 3 tbsps olive oil
- 3 tbsps fresh lime juice, or to taste

Directions:

- Add boiling water into a mixture of salt and couscous in a large sized bowl, and cover it with plastic wrap before letting it stand for about ten minutes.
- In this time, cook unpeeled garlic in hot oil over medium heat until it has turned golden brown.
- Now mash this garlic and add it into the couscous along with black beans, onion, cilantro, corn, jalapeno pepper, olive oil, and lime juice.
- Serve.

Amount per serving (15 total)

Timing Information:

Preparation	Cooking	Total Time
15 min		25 min

Nutritional Information:

Calories	300 kcal
Carbohydrates	44.8 g
Cholesterol	0 mg
Fat	10.9 g
Fiber	3.6 g
Protein	7.1 g
Sodium	713 mg

* Percent Daily Values are based on a 2,000 calorie diet.

Couscous Vi

(Almonds, Raisins, And Lemon)

(Moroccan Style Ii)

Ingredients

- 2 C. water
- 1 C. pearl (Israeli) couscous
- 1 tbsp olive oil
- 1/2 C. chopped yellow onion
- 1 shallot, chopped
- 6 cloves garlic, quartered
- 1/2 C. golden raisins
- 1/2 C. chopped oil-packed sun-dried tomatoes
- 1/2 C. slivered almonds
- 1/2 tsp kosher salt
- 1/4 tsp ground black pepper
- 3 tbsps lemon juice
- 1 tbsp butter, softened

Directions

- Boil your couscous, uncovered for 14 mins in water.
- Simultaneously stir fry your garlic, shallots, and onions for 17 mins in olive oil.
- Now add: almonds, raisins, and tomatoes.
- Cook for 7 more mins.
- Pour the couscous into the shallot mix and cook for 3 mins.
- Add some: lemon juice, pepper, and salt.
- Shut the heat and add in your butter, let it melt, before serving.

- Enjoy.

Amount per serving (6 total)

Timing Information:

Preparation	Cooking	Total Time
10 m	35 m	45 m

Nutritional Information:

Calories	265 kcal
Fat	10.3 g
Carbohydrates	38.6g
Protein	6.6 g
Cholesterol	5 mg
Sodium	208 mg

* Percent Daily Values are based on a 2,000 calorie diet.

Couscous VII

(Jalapenos, Peas, And Mint)

Ingredients

- 2 C. dry couscous
- 1/2 C. chopped green onions
- 1 fresh jalapeno pepper, finely diced
- 2 tbsps olive oil
- 1/2 tsp ground cumin
- 1 pinch cayenne pepper
- 1 pinch ground black pepper
- 2 C. vegetable stock
- 1 bunch asparagus, trimmed and cut into 1/4-inch pieces
- 1 C. shelled fresh or thawed frozen peas
- 2 tbsps chopped fresh mint
- salt and freshly ground black pepper to taste

Directions

- Get a bowl, mix: black pepper, couscous, cayenne, onions, cumin, olive oil, and jalapenos.
- Get your peas and asparagus boiling in the veggie stock and then pour it into the bowl.
- Stir the couscous into the liquid and place a covering on the bowl.
- Let the mix sit for 12 mins then stir it.
- Add some mint, pepper, and salt before serving.
- Enjoy.

Amount per serving (6 total)

Timing Information:

Preparation	Cooking	Total Time
15 m	20 m	35 m

Nutritional Information:

Calories	306 kcal
Fat	5.3 g
Carbohydrates	53.7g
Protein	10.9 g
Cholesterol	0 mg
Sodium	228 mg

* Percent Daily Values are based on a 2,000 calorie diet.

Couscous VIII

(Chicken, Cucumbers, And Parsley)

Ingredients

- 2 C. chicken broth
- 1 (10 oz.) box couscous
- 3/4 C. olive oil
- 1/4 C. fresh lemon juice
- 2 tbsps white balsamic vinegar
- 1/4 C. chopped fresh rosemary leaves
- salt and ground black pepper to taste
- 2 large cooked skinless, boneless chicken breast halves, cut into bite-size pieces
- 1 C. chopped English cucumber
- 1/2 C. chopped sun-dried tomatoes
- 1/2 C. chopped pitted kalamata olives
- 1/2 C. crumbled feta cheese
- 1/3 C. chopped fresh Italian parsley
- salt and ground black pepper to taste

Directions

- Get your stock boiling then add in your couscous.
- Place a lid on the pot and shut the heat.
- Let the contents sit for 7 mins before stirring.
- Blend: vinegar, olive oil, and lemon juice with some rosemary.
- Now add some pepper and salt before continuing.
- Get a bowl, mix: tomatoes, parsley, couscous, feta, cucumbers, and chicken.
- Cover the couscous with the dressing and add a bit more if you like also add some more pepper and salt too.
- Enjoy.

Amount per serving (6 total)

Timing Information:

Preparation	Cooking	Total Time
35 m	10 m	45 m

Nutritional Information:

Calories	645 kcal
Fat	38.8 g
Carbohydrates	44g
Protein	29.4 g
Cholesterol	68 mg
Sodium	792 mg

* Percent Daily Values are based on a 2,000 calorie diet.

Couscous Ix

(Lime And Chicken)

Ingredients

- 1 tbsp olive oil
- 1 lb skinless, boneless chicken breast halves, cubed
- 1 pinch monosodium glutamate (MSG)
- 6 tbsps soy sauce
- 6 tbsps brown sugar
- 1/2 tsp red pepper flakes, or more to taste
- 1 lime, juiced and zested
- 2 C. vegetable broth
- 1 C. couscous
- 1/3 C. chopped cilantro
- 4 wedges lime for garnish

Directions

- Get a bowl, combine: zest, soy sauce, lime juice, sugar, and pepper flakes.
- Boil everything gently for 4 mins until it becomes sauce like.
- Now stir fry your chicken until it is fully done in olive oil for 7 mins.
- Add in your MSG while it fries.
- Then top everything with the lime sauce and continue stir frying for 4 more mins.
- Let your couscous sit in the veggie broth that was boiling for 7 mins in a covered pot.
- Place some couscous on a plate for serving and add a topping of lime chicken.
- Garnish with freshly squeezed lime from the wedges.

- Enjoy.

Amount per serving (4 total)

Timing Information:

Preparation	Cooking	Total Time
15 m	15 m	35 m

Nutritional Information:

Calories	380 kcal
Fat	6.2 g
Carbohydrates	52g
Protein	28.4 g
Cholesterol	59 mg
Sodium	1675 mg

* Percent Daily Values are based on a 2,000 calorie diet.

Couscous X

(Peppers, Corn, And Black Beans)

Ingredients

- 1 C. uncooked couscous
- 1 1/4 C. chicken broth
- 3 tbsps extra virgin olive oil
- 2 tbsps fresh lime juice
- 1 tsp red wine vinegar
- 1/2 tsp ground cumin
- 8 green onions, chopped
- 1 red bell pepper, seeded and chopped
- 1/4 C. chopped fresh cilantro
- 1 C. frozen corn kernels, thawed
- 2 (15 oz.) cans black beans, drained
- salt and pepper to taste

Directions

- Get your broth boiling for 2 mins then add in your couscous.
- Place a lid on the pot and shut the heat.
- Let the couscous sit in the hot water for 7 mins, before stirring it.
- Get a bowl, mix: beans, olive oil, couscous, corn, lime juice, cilantro, vinegar, red pepper, onions, and cumin.
- Add your preferred amount of pepper and salt. Then place a plastic covering around the bowl, let the mix sit in the fridge for 20 to 30 mins before serving.
- Enjoy.

Amount per serving (8 total)

Timing Information:

Preparation	Cooking	Total Time
30 m		35 m

Nutritional Information:

Calories	255 kcal
Fat	5.9 g
Carbohydrates	41.2g
Protein	10.4 g
Cholesterol	< 1 mg
Sodium	565 mg

* Percent Daily Values are based on a 2,000 calorie diet.

Couscous XI

(Creamy Parsley, Chickpeas, And Almonds)

Ingredients

- 1/2 C. creamy salad dressing
- 1/4 C. plain yogurt
- 1 tsp ground cumin
- salt and pepper to taste
- 1 tbsp butter
- 1/2 C. couscous
- 1 C. water
- 1 red onion, chopped
- 1 red bell pepper, chopped
- 1/3 C. chopped parsley
- 1/3 C. raisins
- 1/3 C. toasted and sliced almonds
- 1/2 C. canned chickpeas, drained

Directions

- Get a bowl, combine: pepper, salad dressing, salt, cumin, and yogurt.
- Cover the bowl with some plastic wrap and chill in the fridge for 1 h.
- Simultaneously toast your couscous in butter for 2 mins then add your water.
- Get everything boiling, then place a lid on the pot, set the heat to low and let the contents gently boil for 7 mins.
- Get your dressing mix and add in: chickpeas, couscous, almonds, red onions, raisins, parsley, and bell peppers.

- Place the covering back on the bowl and put it back in the fridge for 20 mins.
- Enjoy.

Amount per serving (6 total)

Timing Information:

Preparation	Cooking	Total Time
15 m	30 m	1 h 45 m

Nutritional Information:

Calories	247 kcal
Fat	12.2 g
Carbohydrates	30g
Protein	5.7 g
Cholesterol	13 mg
Sodium	251 mg

* Percent Daily Values are based on a 2,000 calorie diet.

Couscous XII

(Veggie Turkey Couscous Bits)

Ingredients

- 2 C. coarsely chopped zucchini
- 1 1/2 C. coarsely chopped onions
- 1 red bell pepper, coarsely chopped
- 1 lb extra lean ground turkey
- 1/2 C. uncooked couscous
- 1 egg
- 2 tbsps Worcestershire sauce
- 1 tbsp Dijon mustard
- 1/2 C. barbecue sauce, or as needed

Directions

- Coat your muffin pan with non-stick spray and then set your oven to 400 degrees before doing anything else.
- Blend with a few pulses: bell peppers, zucchini, and onions. Then add them to a bowl, with: mustard, turkey, Worcestershire, eggs, and couscous.
- Evenly divide the mix between the sections in your muffin pan then add bbq sauce to each (1 tsp).
- Cook everything in the oven for 27 mins.
- Check the temperature of each, it should be 160 degrees.
- Let the dish sit for 10 mins before serving.
- Enjoy.

Amount per serving (10 total)

Timing Information:

Preparation	Cooking	Total Time
20 m	25 m	50 m

Nutritional Information:

Calories	119 kcal
Fat	1 g
Carbohydrates	13.6g
Protein	13.2 g
Cholesterol	47 mg
Sodium	244 mg

* Percent Daily Values are based on a 2,000 calorie diet.

Couscous XIII

(Squash And Garbanzos)

(Moroccan Style III)

Ingredients

- 2 tbsps brown sugar
- 1 tbsp butter, melted
- 2 large acorn squash, halved and seeded
- 2 tbsps olive oil
- 2 cloves garlic, chopped
- 2 stalks celery, chopped
- 2 carrots, chopped
- 1 C. garbanzo beans, drained
- 1/2 C. raisins
- 1 1/2 tbsps ground cumin
- salt and pepper to taste
- 1 (14 oz.) can chicken broth
- 1 C. uncooked couscous

Directions

- Set your oven to 350 degrees before doing anything else.
- Cook your squash for 32 mins in the oven. Then top the squash with a mix of butter and sugar that has been melted and stirred together.
- Stir fry, for 7 mins, in olive oil: carrots, celery, and garlic.
- Now add the raisins and beans.
- Fry the contents until everything is soft then add in pepper, salt, and cumin.
- Add the broth to the carrot mix and then add the couscous.

- Place a lid on the pot and place the pot to the side away from all heat.
- Let the contents sit for 7 mins.
- Fill your squashes with the couscous mix.
- Enjoy.

Amount per serving (4 total)

Timing Information:

Preparation	Cooking	Total Time
15 m	45 m	1 h

Nutritional Information:

Calories	502 kcal
Fat	11.7 g
Carbohydrates	93.8g
Protein	11.2 g
Cholesterol	10 mg
Sodium	728 mg

* Percent Daily Values are based on a 2,000 calorie diet.

Couscous XIV

(Cherry Tomatoes, Onions, And Basil)

Ingredients

- 1 C. couscous
- 1 C. boiling water
- 3 tbsps olive oil
- 1 clove garlic, minced
- 1/4 C. diced red bell pepper
- 4 green onions, sliced
- 1 C. cherry tomatoes
- 1 C. fresh basil leaves
- 1 pinch salt
- 1 pinch ground black pepper
- 1 dash balsamic vinegar
- 1/4 C. grated Parmesan cheese

Directions

- Set your oven to 350 degrees before doing anything else.
- Get your water boiling then pour in your couscous.
- Get everything boiling again. Then place a lid on the pot, shut the heat, and let the mix sit for 7 mins before stirring.
- Simultaneously stir fry your peppers, onions, and garlic for 3 mins then add: pepper, tomatoes, salt, basil, and couscous.
- Pour everything into a baking dish and add in your balsamic.
- Cook everything in the oven for 25 mins then add the parmesan.
- Enjoy.

Amount per serving (4 total)

Timing Information:

Preparation	Cooking	Total Time
5 m	35 m	40 m

Nutritional Information:

Calories	299 kcal
Fat	12.4 g
Carbohydrates	38g
Protein	9.1 g
Cholesterol	6 mg
Sodium	196 mg

* Percent Daily Values are based on a 2,000 calorie diet.

Couscous Xv

(Mangos, And Salsa)

Ingredients

- 1 1/2 C. water
- 1 C. couscous
- 2/3 C. dried mango, diced
- 3/4 C. prepared salsa
- 2 tsps ground cumin
- 1 tsp curry powder

Directions

- Get the following boiling in a big pot: curry, couscous, water, cumin, mango, and salsa.
- Place a lid on the pot and set the heat to low.
- Cook everything for 4 mins and then let the contents sit for 7 more mins. Stir the couscous before plating.
- Enjoy.

Amount per serving (4 total)

Timing Information:

Preparation	Cooking	Total Time
10 m	5 m	20 m

Nutritional Information:

Calories	186 kcal
Fat	0.9 g
Carbohydrates	40.2g
Protein	5.1 g

| Cholesterol | 0 mg |
| Sodium | 314 mg |

* Percent Daily Values are based on a 2,000 calorie diet.

Couscous XVI

(Moroccan Salmon Cake)

Ingredients

Mayo Topping:

- 1/2 C. mayonnaise
- 1 clove garlic, crushed
- 1/8 tsp paprika

Salmon Cake:

- 1/2 C. couscous
- 2/3 C. orange juice
- 1 (14.75 oz.) can red salmon, drained
- 1 (10 oz.) package frozen chopped spinach, thawed, drained and squeezed dry
- 2 egg yolks, beaten
- 2 cloves garlic, crushed
- 1 tsp ground cumin
- 1/2 tsp ground black pepper
- 1/2 tsp salt
- 3 tbsps olive oil

Directions

- Get a bowl, mix: paprika, mayo, and garlic.
- Boil your orange juice in a large pot, then add in your couscous.
- Get the mix boiling again and then place a lid on the pot, shut the heat, and let the couscous stand for 7 mins.
- Now stir your couscous after it has lost all of its heat.

- Get a 2nd bowl, combine: salt, salmon, black pepper, spinach, cumin, egg yolks, and garlic.
- Shape this mix into patties and then fry them in olive oil for 8 mins turning each at 4 mins.
- When serving add a topping of mayo.
- Enjoy.

Amount per serving (4 total)

Timing Information:

Preparation	Cooking	Total Time
20 m	25 m	45 m

Nutritional Information:

Calories	620 kcal
Fat	46.4 g
Carbohydrates	26.4g
Protein	28.8 g
Cholesterol	178 mg
Sodium	950 mg

* Percent Daily Values are based on a 2,000 calorie diet.

Couscous XVII

(Feta, Balsamic, And Asparagus)

Ingredients

- 2 C. couscous
- 1 bunch fresh asparagus, trimmed and cut into 2-inch pieces
- 8 oz. grape tomatoes, halved
- 6 oz. feta cheese, crumbled
- 3 tbsps balsamic vinegar
- 2 tbsps extra-virgin olive oil
- Black pepper, to taste

Directions

- Boil your couscous in water, then place a lid on the pot, shut the heat, and let the couscous sit for 7 mins.
- Once it has cooled stir it with a fork.
- Simultaneously steam your asparagus over 2 inches of boiling water with a steamer insert and a pot. Steam the spears for 7 mins. Now remove all the liquid.
- Get a bowl, toss: couscous, olive oil, asparagus, balsamic, cheese, pepper, and tomatoes.
- Enjoy chilled or warm.

Amount per serving (4 total)

Timing Information:

Preparation	Cooking	Total Time
10 m	20 m	30 m

Nutritional Information:

Calories	541 kcal
Fat	16.7 g
Carbohydrates	77.7g
Protein	20.1 g
Cholesterol	38 mg
Sodium	494 mg

* Percent Daily Values are based on a 2,000 calorie diet.

Couscous XVIII

(Peppers, Cucumbers, And Olives)

(Greek Style Ii)

Ingredients

- 3 (6 oz.) packages garlic and herb couscous mix
- 1 pint cherry tomatoes, cut in half
- 1 (5 oz.) jar pitted kalamata olives, halved
- 1 C. mixed bell peppers (green, red, yellow, orange), diced
- 1 cucumber, sliced and then halved
- 1/2 C. parsley, finely chopped
- 1 (8 oz.) package crumbled feta cheese
- 1/2 C. Greek vinaigrette salad dressing

Directions

- Get your couscous boiling in water for 2 mins. Then place a lid on the pot, shut and heat, and it sit for 7 mins before stirring after it has cooled.
- Place the couscous in a bowl, and combine in: cheese, tomatoes, parsley, olives, cucumber, and bell peppers.
- Add in your Greek dressing and toss everything to coat evenly.
- Feel free to add more dressing if you like.
- Enjoy.

Amount per serving (20 total)

Timing Information:

Preparation	Cooking	Total Time
30 m	15 m	45 m

Nutritional Information:

Calories	159 kcal
Fat	6.5 g
Carbohydrates	21.4g
Protein	5.7 g
Cholesterol	10 mg
Sodium	642 mg

* Percent Daily Values are based on a 2,000 calorie diet.

Couscous XIX

(Cloves, Onions, Tomatoes, And Chicken)

(Moroccan Style Iv)

Ingredients

- 1 C. whole wheat couscous
- 1 tbsp vegetable oil
- 1 medium onion, chopped
- 2 bay leaves
- 5 whole cloves, crushed
- 1/2 tsp cinnamon
- 1 tsp ground dried turmeric
- 1/4 tsp ground cayenne pepper
- 6 skinless, boneless chicken breast halves - chopped
- 1 (16 oz.) can garbanzo beans
- 1 (16 oz.) can crushed tomatoes
- 1 (48 fluid oz.) can chicken broth
- 2 carrots, cut into 1/2 inch pieces
- 1 zucchini, cut into 1/2-inch pieces
- salt to taste

Directions

- Get your couscous boiling in water for 2 mins. Then place a lid on the pot, shut and heat, and it sit for 7 mins before stirring once it has cooled.
- Stir fry your onions in oil until soft then add in: cayenne, bay leaves, turmeric, cloves, and cinnamon.
- Cook everything for 1 more min then pour in your chicken and cook it until browned all over.

- Once everything has been browned add in: broth, tomatoes, and beans.
- Get everything boiling.
- Lower the heat to low and gently boil for 27 mins.
- Now add your zucchini and carrots and also some salt.
- Continue for 12 more mins.
- Serve the veggies and chicken over the couscous.
- Enjoy.

Amount per serving (6 total)

Timing Information:

Preparation	Cooking	Total Time
15 m	45 m	1 h

Nutritional Information:

Calories	399 kcal
Fat	6.7 g
Carbohydrates	50.7g
Protein	33.4 g
Cholesterol	67 mg
Sodium	1539 mg

* Percent Daily Values are based on a 2,000 calorie diet.

Couscous Xx

(Almonds, Cilantro, And Curry)

Ingredients

- 1 1/2 C. couscous
- 3 C. chicken stock
- 1 tbsp curry powder
- 2 tsps salt
- 1 tsp ground black pepper
- 2 tbsps extra-virgin olive oil
- 1/2 C. raisins
- 1 bunch cilantro, chopped
- 1/2 C. slivered almonds, toasted

Directions

- Boil the following then pour it over your couscous in a salad bowl: raisins, stock, olive oil, curry powder, pepper, and salt.
- Place some plastic wrap around the bowl, and let the couscous stand for 12 mins before stirring it.
- Serve the couscous with some almonds and cilantro.
- Enjoy.

Amount per serving (6 total)

Timing Information:

Preparation	Cooking	Total Time
10 m	10 m	30 m

Nutritional Information:

Calories	269 kcal
Fat	9.8 g
Carbohydrates	39.4g
Protein	7.1 g
Cholesterol	< 1 mg
Sodium	1131 mg

* Percent Daily Values are based on a 2,000 calorie diet.

Couscous XXI

(Spicy Chicken And Carrots)

Ingredients

- 3 1/4 C. low-sodium chicken broth
- 1 C. quick-cooking couscous
- 2 tbsps olive oil
- 4 skinless, boneless chicken breast halves - cut into cubes
- 1 pinch ground black pepper
- 1/2 C. finely chopped jalapeno chili peppers
- 1 carrot, thinly sliced
- 1 zucchini, diced
- 3 green onions, thinly sliced
- 1 1/2 tsps grated fresh ginger root
- 1 1/2 tsps curry powder
- 1/2 tsp ground coriander seed
- 1 tsp cornstarch

Directions

- Boil your broth (2 C.) and then add the couscous and olive oil. Place a lid on the pot and let the contents sit for 12 mins.
- Get a bowl, mix: cornstarch, 1 C. of broth, and curry.
- Coat your chicken with pepper then stir fry it in 1 tbsp of olive oil until fully done.
- Remove the chicken from the pan.
- Add in more olive oil and stir fry carrots and jalapenos for 4 mins then add: a quarter of a C. of broth, zucchini, ginger, and onions.
- Cook everything for 7 more mins.
- Add your cornstarch mix and cook for 3 more mins.

- Serve the spicy chicken and carrots over the couscous.
- Enjoy.

Amount per serving (4 total)

Timing Information:

Preparation	Cooking	Total Time
20 m	25 m	45 m

Nutritional Information:

Calories	415 kcal
Fat	11.5 g
Carbohydrates	40.6g
Protein	35.8 g
Cholesterol	75 mg
Sodium	177 mg

* Percent Daily Values are based on a 2,000 calorie diet.

Couscous XXII

(Peppers, Shrimp, And Feta)

Ingredients

- 2 C. couscous
- 2 C. water
- 3/4 C. olive oil
- 1/4 C. apple cider vinegar
- 1 tsp Dijon mustard
- 1 tsp ground cumin
- 1 clove garlic, crushed
- salt and pepper to taste
- 1 red bell pepper, chopped
- 1 yellow bell pepper, chopped
- 1 1/2 lbs cooked shrimp, peeled and deveined
- 2 medium tomatoes, chopped
- 1 C. chopped fresh parsley
- 1 C. crumbled feta cheese

Directions

- Boil your water then pour in your couscous, place a lid on the pot, and then let it sit for 7 mins and finally stir it once cooled.
- Get a bowl, combine: pepper, olive oil, salt, garlic, vinegar, and mustard.
- Get a bigger bowl, mix: cheese, shrimp, parsley, couscous, tomatoes, and bell peppers.
- Now combine in the vinegar mix and toss everything to coat.
- Place the mix in the fridge for 1 hr then serve.
- Enjoy.

Amount per serving (8 total)

Timing Information:

Preparation	Cooking	Total Time
30 m	5 m	35 m

Nutritional Information:

Calories	530 kcal
Fat	28.4 g
Carbohydrates	38.7g
Protein	28.7 g
Cholesterol	194 mg
Sodium	570 mg

* Percent Daily Values are based on a 2,000 calorie diet.

Couscous XXIII

(Pepper, Lemon, And Cilantro)

Ingredients

- 2 tbsps butter
- 2 tbsps olive oil
- 4 (4 oz.) salmon steaks
- 1 tsp minced garlic
- 1 tbsp lemon pepper
- 1 tsp salt
- 1/4 C. water
- 1 C. chopped fresh tomatoes
- 1 C. chopped fresh cilantro
- 2 C. boiling water
- 1 C. uncooked couscous

Directions

- Coat your salmon with salt, lemon pepper, and garlic.
- Now begin cooking it in olive oil and butter.
- Then add a quarter of a C. of water, cilantro, and tomatoes. Place a lid on the pan and cook for 16 mins.
- Simultaneously boil 2 C. of water then add in the couscous. Place a lid on the pot and the couscous stand for 7 mins.
- Top your salmon and couscous with any sauce in the pan when serving.
- Enjoy.

Amount per serving (4 total)

Timing Information:

Preparation	Cooking	Total Time
10 m	20 m	30 m

Nutritional Information:

Calories	498 kcal
Fat	23.5 g
Carbohydrates	36.2g
Protein	31.6 g
Cholesterol	89 mg
Sodium	1039 mg

* Percent Daily Values are based on a 2,000 calorie diet.

Couscous XXIV

(Lemons, Parsley, Basil, Lettuce)

Ingredients

- 10 oz. uncooked couscous
- 2 tbsps olive oil
- 1/2 C. lemon juice
- 3/4 tsp salt
- 1/4 tsp ground black pepper
- 1 cucumber, seeded and chopped
- 1/2 C. finely chopped green onions
- 1/2 C. fresh parsley, chopped
- 1/4 C. fresh basil, chopped
- 6 leaves lettuce
- 6 slices lemon

Directions

- Boil 1 and 3/4 C. of water then pour in the couscous.
- Let it boil for 2 mins before placing a lid on the pan and setting it to the side for 7 mins.
- Stir the contents after it has cooled off a bit.
- Get a bowl, mix: pepper, oil, salt, cucumber, couscous, onions, basil, parsley, and lemon juice.
- Serve the couscous over leaves of fresh lettuce and add some lemon as a topping on each plate.
- Enjoy.

Amount per serving (8 total)

Timing Information:

Preparation	Cooking	Total Time
10 m	10 m	1 h 20 m

Nutritional Information:

Calories	142 kcal
Fat	3.6 g
Carbohydrates	24.6g
Protein	4 g
Cholesterol	0 mg
Sodium	227 mg

* Percent Daily Values are based on a 2,000 calorie diet.

Couscous XXV

(Creamy Mushrooms And Pork)

Ingredients

- 1 tbsp vegetable oil
- 4 boneless pork chops, 3/4-inch thick
- 1 clove garlic, minced
- 1 (10.75 oz.) can Cream of Mushroom Soup
- 1/2 C. milk
- 4 C. hot cooked couscous or regular long-grain white rice

Directions

- Stir fry your pork for 12 mins in oil and then remove it from the pan.
- Add in your milk and soup and heat it until everything is boiling.
- Once it is boiling put the pork back in the pan and lower your heat to a simmer.
- Cook everything covered for 12 mins or until the pork is completely done.
- Enjoy over the couscous.

Amount per serving (4 total)

Timing Information:

Preparation	Cooking	Total Time
25 m		25 m

Nutritional Information:

Calories	376 kcal
Fat	11.1 g
Carbohydrates	40.1g
Protein	27.4 g
Cholesterol	66 mg
Sodium	463 mg

* Percent Daily Values are based on a 2,000 calorie diet.

Couscous XXVI

(Breakfast I)

Ingredients

- 2 C. skim milk
- 2 tbsps honey
- 3 tsps ground cinnamon
- 2 C. dry couscous
- 1/3 C. chopped dried apricots
- 1/3 C. raisins
- 1/2 C. slivered almonds

Directions

- Get the following boiling: cinnamon, honey, and milk.
- Add in the couscous and place a lid on the pot.
- Place the contents to the side away from the heat and let it sit for 7 mins.
- Now add your almonds, raisins, and apricots before serving.
- Enjoy.

Amount per serving (8 total)

Timing Information:

Preparation	Cooking	Total Time
5 m	5 m	10 m

Nutritional Information:

Calories	286 kcal
Fat	4.9 g

Carbohydrates	52.1g
Protein	9.9 g
Cholesterol	1 mg
Sodium	32 mg

* Percent Daily Values are based on a 2,000 calorie diet.

Couscous XXVII

(Apricots, Raisins, Almonds, And Dates)

(Moroccan Style V)

Ingredients

- 2 C. vegetable broth
- 5 tbsps unsalted butter
- 1/3 C. chopped dates
- 1/3 C. chopped dried apricots
- 1/3 C. golden raisins
- 2 C. dry couscous
- 3 tsps ground cinnamon
- 1/2 C. slivered almonds, toasted

Directions

- Get your broth boiling and then add in: raisins, butter, dates, and apricots.
- Continue the gentle boil for 4 more mins.
- Then add the couscous and a lid to the pot.
- Place everything to the side for 7 mins.
- Add your almonds that have been toasted for a few mins and your cinnamon.
- Stir the mix and then plate.
- Enjoy.

Amount per serving (6 total)

Timing Information:

Preparation	Cooking	Total Time
15 m	5 m	20 m

Nutritional Information:

Calories	442 kcal
Fat	14.8 g
Carbohydrates	68.2g
Protein	10.5 g
Cholesterol	25 mg
Sodium	164 mg

* Percent Daily Values are based on a 2,000 calorie diet.

Couscous XXVIII

(Garlic, Roma Tomatoes, And Monterey)

Ingredients

- 1 (10 oz.) box couscous
- 1 1/2 C. boiling water
- 2 tbsps olive oil
- 1/2 onion, diced
- 2 cloves garlic, minced
- 3 Roma (plum) tomatoes, diced
- 1/2 C. shredded Cheddar-Monterey Jack cheese blend

Directions

- Get a pot and boil your water in it. Pour it over your couscous in a bowl, and place a covering over everything.
- Let the contents sit for 12 mins.
- Once the couscous has cooled stir it.
- At the same time stir fry your garlic and onions for 7 mins then add in the tomatoes and cook until the juice of the tomatoes begins to become thick.
- Add in the couscous as well as the cheese, and cook for 2 more mins or until the cheese has melted.
- Plate and serve.
- Enjoy.

Amount per serving (4 total)

Timing Information:

Preparation	Cooking	Total Time
20 m	10 m	30 m

Nutritional Information:

Calories	399 kcal
Fat	11.3 g
Carbohydrates	60.4g
Protein	12.9 g
Cholesterol	12 mg
Sodium	99 mg

* Percent Daily Values are based on a 2,000 calorie diet.

Couscous XXVIII

(Tomatoes, Mozzarella, Basil, And Mint)

Ingredients

- 4 large tomatoes
- 1 1/2 C. vegetable broth
- 1/2 C. sun-dried tomatoes, chopped
- 1 C. couscous
- 1/4 C. shredded nonfat mozzarella cheese
- 1/4 C. chopped fresh basil
- 2 tbsps minced fresh mint leaves
- 1/4 tsp ground black pepper

Directions

- Set your oven to 375 degrees before doing anything else.
- Divide your tomatoes in two, then remove the inside flesh and place them to the side.
- Invert the skins and let them dry out on a working surface.
- While the tomatoes are drying boil the sun dried tomatoes in broth for 4 mins then pour in the couscous.
- Place a lid on the pot and shut the heat.
- Let the couscous sit for 7 mins.
- Add to your couscous: pepper, cheese, tomato insides, mint, and basil.
- Mix everything evenly. Then fill up your tomato skins with the mix.
- Put the stuffed tomatoes in a casserole dish and cook them in the oven for 32 mins.
- Enjoy.

Amount per serving (4 total)

Timing Information:

Preparation	Cooking	Total Time
25 m	30 m	55 m

Nutritional Information:

Calories	245 kcal
Fat	1.1 g
Carbohydrates	47.7g
Protein	11.4 g
Cholesterol	1 mg
Sodium	284 mg

* Percent Daily Values are based on a 2,000 calorie diet.

Couscous Xxx

(Almonds, Ham, Ginger, And Broccoli)

Ingredients

- 1 1/2 C. water
- 1 C. couscous
- 2 C. chicken broth
- 1/4 C. cornstarch
- 3 tbsps soy sauce
- 3 tbsps brown sugar
- 1/8 tsp ground ginger
- 1 tbsp vegetable oil
- 2 cloves garlic, minced
- 1 (16 oz.) package mixed broccoli and cauliflower florets
- 1 carrot, sliced
- 1/4 lb cooked ham, cut into strips
- 1 (8 oz.) can sliced water chestnuts, drained
- 1/2 C. sliced almonds

Directions

- Get your couscous boiling in water for 12 mins. Then place a lid on the pot and shut the heat.
- Get a bowl, mix: ginger, broth, sugar, soy sauce, and cornstarch.
- Stir fry the following in veggie oil for 9 mins: carrots, garlic, cauliflower, and broccoli.
- Pour in the soy sauce mix and cook for 1 min. Then add the chestnuts and ham, cook for 2 more mins, while stirring, and then add in the almonds.
- Enjoy the veggies alongside or over the couscous.

Amount per serving (6 total)

Timing Information:

Preparation	Cooking	Total Time
10 m	10 m	20 m

Nutritional Information:

Calories	318 kcal
Fat	8.9 g
Carbohydrates	46.6g
Protein	12.9 g
Cholesterol	11 mg
Sodium	994 mg

* Percent Daily Values are based on a 2,000 calorie diet.

Couscous XXXI

(Feta, Cucumbers, Jalapenos, Basil, And Cilantro)

Ingredients

- 3 C. water
- 2 C. couscous
- 1/2 C. crumbled feta cheese
- 1 fresh jalapeno pepper, chopped
- 1/2 cucumber, diced
- 1 clove garlic, minced
- 1/2 C. chopped green onion
- 3 tbsps chopped fresh mint
- 3 tbsps chopped fresh basil
- 3 tbsps chopped fresh cilantro
- 1 tbsp chopped fresh parsley
- 2 tsps ground cumin
- 2 tsps cayenne pepper
- 1 lemon, juiced

Directions

- Boil your couscous in water for 2 mins, then place a lid on the pot, shut the heat, and let it sit for 7 to 10 mins.
- Once it has cooled and all the liquid has been soaked up stir the mix with a fork.
- Simultaneously add the following to a salad bowl: lemon juice, cheese, cayenne, jalapenos, cumin, cucumbers, garlic, parsley, onions, cilantro, basil, and mint.
- Mix the couscous in with other ingredients after it has finished cooking and also has cooled.

- Enjoy.

Amount per serving (6 total)

Timing Information:

Preparation	Cooking	Total Time
20 m	10 m	30 m

Nutritional Information:

Calories	210 kcal
Fat	3.3 g
Carbohydrates	38.3g
Protein	8.1 g
Cholesterol	11 mg
Sodium	155 mg

* Percent Daily Values are based on a 2,000 calorie diet.

Couscous XXXII

(Peppers, Garlic, Onions, Mushrooms, And Dates)

Ingredients

- 1 tbsp olive oil
- 1 medium onion, chopped
- 2 whole star anise pods
- salt to taste
- 3 cloves garlic, peeled and chopped
- 1/2 red bell pepper, chopped
- 2 dried hot red peppers, diced
- 1/2 tsp ground black pepper
- 4 large fresh mushrooms, chopped
- 1 tbsp lemon juice
- 1/4 C. chopped dates
- 1 tsp ground cinnamon
- 1 C. uncooked couscous
- 1 1/2 C. vegetable stock

Directions

- Stir fry your onions until soft then add in some salt and anise. Add the black pepper, garlic, hot red peppers and bell pepper too.
- Continue stir frying until these peppers become soft. Now add in the lemon juice, cinnamon, mushrooms, and dates.
- Let the date mix cook for 12 mins with a low level of heat.
- Meanwhile gently boil your couscous in the stock, in a lidded pot, for 7 mins. Then stir the couscous after it has cooled off slightly.

- Pour the stirred couscous into the date mix and stir everything.
- Enjoy.

Amount per serving (2 total)

Timing Information:

Preparation	Cooking	Total Time
10 m	20 m	30 m

Nutritional Information:

Calories	594 kcal
Fat	10.6 g
Carbohydrates	111.9g
Protein	18 g
Cholesterol	0 mg
Sodium	315 mg

* Percent Daily Values are based on a 2,000 calorie diet.

Couscous XXXIII

(Cucumbers, Capers, And Dates)

Ingredients

- 1 skinless, boneless chicken breast half
- 1/2 C. couscous
- 1/2 C. water
- 1 tbsp unsalted butter
- 1 pinch salt
- 1 tbsp salted butter
- 1/4 C. capers, drained
- 3 dates, pitted and chopped
- 1/4 C. mascarpone cheese
- 1/4 C. heavy cream
- salt and ground black pepper to taste (optional)
- 1 date, pitted and chopped
- 1/4 cucumber, diced
- 1/2 tomato, diced
- 1 tsp lemon juice (optional)

Directions

- Grill your chicken for 7 mins per side. Then divide it into two pieces.
- Boil your water with some salt and butter. Then pour in the couscous, place a lid on the pot, shut the heat to the stove, and let the contents sit for 12 mins.
- Let it cool and then stir it.
- Stir fry your dates and capers for a few mins in the butter then add in the cream and the cheese. Let the cheese mix cook for 4 mins.

- Place your couscous on serving platter add a diced date and then some cheese sauce and then the chicken.
- Add some chopped tomatoes and cucumber with some lemon juice as well.
- Enjoy.

Amount per serving (2 total)

Timing Information:

Preparation	Cooking	Total Time
30 m	25 m	55 m

Nutritional Information:

Calories	616 kcal
Fat	37.5 g
Carbohydrates	50.6g
Protein	21.9 g
Cholesterol	140 mg
Sodium	616 mg

* Percent Daily Values are based on a 2,000 calorie diet.

Couscous XXXIV

(Kebabs)

(Moroccan Style VI

Ingredients

- 1 (8 oz.) package tempeh, cut into 1/2 inch squares
- 16 fresh white mushrooms
- 1 medium eggplant, cut into 1 inch cubes
- 1 large red bell pepper, cut into 1 inch pieces
- 16 cherry tomatoes
- 8 tbsps olive oil
- 4 tbsps soy sauce
- 4 tbsps teriyaki sauce
- 3 tbsps honey
- 1 tbsp grated fresh ginger root
- 1 tbsp chopped fresh garlic
- salt and pepper to taste
- 2 C. vegetable broth
- 1 tbsp grated fresh ginger root
- 1 tsp ground cumin
- salt to taste
- 1 C. dry couscous
- 3/4 C. raisins
- 3/4 C. drained canned chick-peas (garbanzo beans)
- 1 lemon

Directions

- Get a bowl, combine the following: black pepper, tomatoes, olive oil, bell peppers, salt, soy sauce, eggplants, garlic (1

tbsp), tempeh, teriyaki sauce, ginger (1 tbsp), mushrooms, and honey.
- Place plastic wrap around the bowl and place everything in the fridge for 1 to 2 hours.
- Get the following boiling: salt, veggie stock, cumin, and ginger (1 tbsp).
- Once boiling pour in your couscous, beans, and raisins.
- Place a lid on the pot, shut the heat, and leave it for 7 mins.
- Once the couscous has cooled, add some fresh squeezed lemon juice over it.
- Stake your veggies on skewers and then grill them until the veggies are done, and have grill marks.
- Serve your kebabs with the couscous.

NOTE: If you prefer to not use a grill you can cook the kebabs under the broiler.

Amount per serving (4 total)

Timing Information:

Preparation	Cooking	Total Time
30 m	15 m	2 h 45 m

Nutritional Information:

Calories	820 kcal
Fat	35.3 g
Carbohydrates	110.1g
Protein	26.8 g
Cholesterol	0 mg
Sodium	2132 mg

* Percent Daily Values are based on a 2,000 calorie diet.

Couscous Xxxv

(Carrots, Harissa, Peppers, Chicken, And Sausage)

Ingredients

- 3 tbsp olive oil
- 2 lbs chicken thighs
- 12 oz. Italian sausage
- 1 tbsp diced garlic
- 2 onions, minced
- 2 carrots, julienned
- 1/2 stalk celery, chunked
- 1 rutabaga, parsnip, or turnip, chunked
- 1/2 green bell pepper, julienned
- 1/2 red bell pepper, julienned
- 1 can diced tomatoes
- 1 can garbanzo beans
- 2 C. chicken stock
- 2 tsps thyme
- 1 tsp turmeric
- 1 tsp cayenne pepper
- 1/4 tsp harissa
- 1 bay leaf
- 2 zucchini, cut in half
- 2 C. couscous
- 2 C. chicken stock
- 1/2 C. plain yogurt

Directions

- Brown your chicken thighs all over in olive oil.

- Add in your sausage and cook everything until fully done. Once it has cooled dice the sausage into pieces.
- Now stir fry your garlic and onions until tender and see-through then combine in: stock, bay leaf, carrots, harissa, beans, celery, cayenne, tomatoes, turmeric, rutabaga, thyme, red and green peppers.
- Cook for 2 more mins before adding your chicken and sausage.
- Place a lid on the pan and cook for 35 mins until chicken is fully done.
- Add your zucchini and cook for 7 more mins.
- Meanwhile boil 2 C. of chicken stock then pour it over your couscous in a bowl along with 2 tbsps of olive oil.
- Place a covering on the bowl and let it sit for at least 10 mins.
- When plating the dish first layer couscous then some chicken mix and then some yogurt.
- Enjoy.

Amount per serving (6 total)

Timing Information:

Preparation	Cooking	Total Time
45 m	45 m	1 h 30 m

Nutritional Information:

Calories	934 kcal
Fat	39 g
Carbohydrates	80.5g
Protein	62.2 g
Cholesterol	169 mg
Sodium	601 mg

* Percent Daily Values are based on a 2,000 calorie diet.

Couscous XXXVI

(Garlic, Kale, And Parmesan)

Ingredients

- 1 C. water
- 2 tbsps butter
- 1 C. whole wheat couscous
- 2 tbsps extra-virgin olive oil
- 1 (15 oz.) can cannellini beans, drained and rinsed
- 1 C. chopped kale
- 4 cloves garlic, chopped
- 1/4 C. whole salted almonds, halved
- 1/4 C. grated Parmesan cheese
- salt and freshly ground black pepper to taste

Directions

- Boil your couscous in butter and water.
- Once boiling place a lid on the pot, shut the heat, and let it stand for 7 mins.
- Once it has cooled off stir the mix with a fork.
- Stir fry garlic, kale, and beans in olive oil for 9 mins.
- Combine the bean mix with the couscous and then add the almonds.
- Add your preferred amount of pepper and salt and then garnish your servings with parmesan.
- Enjoy.

Amount per serving (4 total)

Timing Information:

Preparation	Cooking	Total Time
15 m	5 m	25 m

Nutritional Information:

Calories	432 kcal
Fat	19.2 g
Carbohydrates	51.1g
Protein	13.9 g
Cholesterol	20 mg
Sodium	352 mg

* Percent Daily Values are based on a 2,000 calorie diet.

Couscous XXXVII

(Savory, Parsley, Lemon, And Tomatoes)

Ingredients

- 1 C. water
- 1 tsp dried savory
- 1 tsp dried parsley
- 1 pinch crushed red pepper flakes
- 1 tbsp chicken bouillon granules
- 1/2 C. pearl (Israeli) couscous
- 1 lemon, zest grated
- 1/2 C. toasted slivered almonds
- 1/2 C. chopped celery
- 1/3 C. chopped onion
- 1/2 tomato, seeded and chopped
- 1 tbsp olive oil
- salt and black pepper to taste

Directions

- Boil: bouillon, savory, pepper flakes, and parsley.
- Once boiling add in the couscous.
- Set the heat to low and let the contents gently boil for 12 mins.
- Place a lid on the pot and let everything cool and remove any extra liquid.
- Pour everything into a big bowl and add: olive oil, zest, tomatoes, salt, almonds, black pepper, onions, and celery.
- Place a wrapping of foil around the bowl and leave it in the fridge for 2 hrs before serving.
- Enjoy.

Amount per serving (3 total)

Timing Information:

Preparation	Cooking	Total Time
20 m	10 m	1 h 30 m

Nutritional Information:

Calories	266 kcal
Fat	14.3 g
Carbohydrates	27g
Protein	7.9 g
Cholesterol	< 1 mg
Sodium	401 mg

* Percent Daily Values are based on a 2,000 calorie diet.

Couscous XXXVIII

(Buttery Chives And Cheddar)

Ingredients

- 2 tsps butter
- 1 C. pearl (Israeli) couscous
- 2 C. chicken broth
- 1/2 C. heavy cream
- 1/4 C. diced pimientos
- 1 pinch cayenne pepper, or more to taste
- 3 oz. shredded sharp Cheddar cheese
- 1 tbsp chopped fresh chives
- salt and freshly ground black pepper to taste

Directions

- Toast your couscous in butter for 3 mins.
- Then add the broth and get everything boiling.
- Set the heat to its lowest level and let the couscous gently boil for 9 mins.
- Add the following to the couscous: cayenne, pimientos, and cream.
- Cook for 4 more mins, if the mix becomes too dry add more broth.
- Shut the heat and add in your cheddar and let it melt before adding in the chives and a bit more pepper and salt.
- Enjoy.

Amount per serving (4 total)

Timing Information:

Preparation	Cooking	Total Time
15 m	10 m	25 m

Nutritional Information:

Calories	358 kcal
Fat	20.6 g
Carbohydrates	31.3g
Protein	11.4 g
Cholesterol	71 mg
Sodium	740 mg

* Percent Daily Values are based on a 2,000 calorie diet.

Couscous Xxxix

(Tomatoes And Tarragon)

Ingredients

- 1 C. couscous
- 1 1/8 C. boiling chicken stock
- water to cover
- 2 tbsps butter
- 4 skinless, boneless chicken breast halves
- 2/3 C. heavy whipping cream
- 1/2 C. sweet corn
- 2 tomatoes, chopped
- 1/4 C. fresh chopped tarragon
- salt and pepper to taste
- 1/2 lemon, juiced

Directions

- Simmer for 4 mins, your couscous, in water and half of the stock.
- Shut the heat and place a lid on the pot.
- Stir fry your chicken in butter with the rest of the stock and cream until bubbly.
- Now add the tarragon, tomatoes, and corn, cook for 2 mins, before adding lemon juice, pepper and salt.
- Layer each plate with couscous and then the chicken mix.
- Enjoy.

Amount per serving (4 total)

Timing Information:

Preparation	Cooking	Total Time
10 m	30 m	40 m

Nutritional Information:

Calories	505 kcal
Fat	23.7 g
Carbohydrates	42.8g
Protein	30.8 g
Cholesterol	131 mg
Sodium	368 mg

* Percent Daily Values are based on a 2,000 calorie diet.

Couscous XL

(Pine Nuts, Currants, And Pork)

Ingredients

- 1 1/2 C. reduced-sodium chicken broth, divided
- 5 tbsps butter, divided
- 3/4 C. dry couscous
- 1 small onion, finely chopped
- 2 cloves garlic, minced
- 1/2 C. currants
- 1/2 C. pine nuts
- 1/8 tsp ground cinnamon
- salt and freshly ground black pepper
- 6 boneless pork loin chops, butterflied
- 1/2 C. orange marmalade

Directions

- Boil your couscous in butter (2 tbsps) and broth (1 1/4 C.) for 2 mins then shut the heat, add a lid to the pot, and let it sit for 12 mins. Once it has cooled, stir it.
- Now stir fry your garlic and onions in butter (3 tbsps) for 7 mins.
- Place the pan to the side and add in: salt, cinnamon, pepper, currants, couscous, and pine nuts.
- Add a bit more stock so that mix can be held together and then set your oven to 350 degrees before doing anything else.
- Fill your pork pieces with the couscous mix and stake each one with a tooth pick.

- Put everything in a casserole dish that has been coated with nonstick spray and coat them with the marmalade.
- Cook the pork in the oven for 47 mins then take out the toothpicks.
- Enjoy.

Amount per serving (6 total)

Timing Information:

Preparation	Cooking	Total Time
35 m	45 m	1 h 20 m

Nutritional Information:

Calories	500 kcal
Fat	23.1 g
Carbohydrates	46.6g
Protein	28.7 g
Cholesterol	85 mg
Sodium	151 mg

* Percent Daily Values are based on a 2,000 calorie diet.

Couscous XLI

(Bacon, Balsamic, And Curry)

Ingredients

- 4 slices bacon
- 1 onion, chopped
- 1 1/2 C. water
- 1 C. uncooked couscous
- 3/4 C. diced carrot
- 3/4 C. diced cucumber
- 1/2 red bell pepper, diced
- 1/2 (15 oz.) can garbanzo beans, drained and rinsed
- 1/4 C. olive oil
- 2 tbsps white balsamic vinegar
- 1 tbsp soy sauce
- 1 tbsp white sugar
- 2 tsps curry powder
- salt and pepper to taste

Directions

- Stir fry your bacon for 11 mins and place everything on paper towels.
- Now stir fry your onions in bacon drippings and then set it to the side.
- Boil your couscous in water. Then place a lid on it and let it sit for 7 mins before stirring it after it has cooled.
- Get a bowl, combine: beans, onions, bell peppers, carrots, and cucumbers.
- Get a 2nd bowl, combine: pepper, olive oil, salt, vinegar, curry, soy sauce, and sugar.

- Top the couscous with the dressing mix and add the bacon bits.
- Enjoy.

Amount per serving (8 total)

Timing Information:

Preparation	Cooking	Total Time
25 m	5 m	50 m

Nutritional Information:

Calories	212 kcal
Fat	9.1 g
Carbohydrates	26.6g
Protein	5.9 g
Cholesterol	5 mg
Sodium	283 mg

* Percent Daily Values are based on a 2,000 calorie diet.

Couscous XLII

(Pecans, Parmesan, And Pesto)

Ingredients

- 2/3 C. pecan pieces
- 1 tbsp butter
- 1 1/2 C. quartered fresh button mushrooms
- 1 onion, chopped
- 1 tbsp minced fresh garlic
- 2 tsps butter
- 1 1/4 C. water
- 1 (5.8 oz.) box couscous
- 1 (8.5 oz.) bottle sun-dried tomato pesto
- 1/3 C. finely grated Parmesan cheese, or more to taste
- salt and ground black pepper to taste

Directions

- Toast your pecans in the oven in a casserole dish for 25 mins.
- Meanwhile stir fry the garlic, onions, and mushrooms in 1 tbsp of butter for 9 mins. Then place it all in a bowl.
- Melt 2 more tbsp of butter and then add in your water get it boiling.
- Once everything is boiling add your couscous to a big bowl and then combine it with the boiling water.
- Place a covering on the bowl of plastic wrap and let it sit for 12 mins.
- After all the liquid has been absorbed stir it with a fork.
- Add the pesto, pecans, parmesan, and mushrooms to the couscous and then add some pepper and salt.
- Mix everything evenly.

- Enjoy.

Amount per serving (4 total)

Timing Information:

Preparation	Cooking	Total Time
20 m	30 m	50 m

Nutritional Information:

Calories	471 kcal
Fat	31.3 g
Carbohydrates	38.8g
Protein	11.3 g
Cholesterol	19 mg
Sodium	222 mg

* Percent Daily Values are based on a 2,000 calorie diet.

Couscous XLIII

(Honey Rutabaga)

Ingredients

- 1 rutabaga, chunked
- 2 C. water
- 1 tbsp vegetable oil
- 1 1/2 C. couscous
- 1/2 C. nutritional yeast
- 1/4 C. vegetable oil
- 1/4 C. apple cider vinegar
- 1 1/2 tsps honey
- 1 tsp Italian seasoning
- 1 tsp dried oregano
- 1 tsp dried dill weed
- 1/2 tsp ground black pepper
- 1/4 tsp cayenne pepper
- 1 pinch salt to taste (optional)

Directions

- Steam your rutabaga over 2 inches of boiling water for 12 mins with a steamer insert.
- Boil 1 tbsp of veggie oil with 2 C. of water then add in the couscous and shut the heat after placing a lid on the pot.
- Let this sit for 15 mins before stirring after it has cooled.
- Get a bowl, combine: cayenne, veggie oil, black pepper, vinegar, dill, honey, oregano, and Italian seasonings.
- Add the rutabaga, couscous, and some salt to the dressing mix.
- Toss the contents to coat everything evenly.

- Enjoy.

Amount per serving (6 total)

Timing Information:

Preparation	Cooking	Total Time
15 m	20 m	35 m

Nutritional Information:

Calories	330 kcal
Fat	12.3 g
Carbohydrates	44.2g
Protein	11.7 g
Cholesterol	0 mg
Sodium	89 mg

* Percent Daily Values are based on a 2,000 calorie diet.

Couscous XLIV

(Green Beans And Black Beans)

Ingredients

- 2 tsps vegetable oil
- 1 medium onion, chopped
- 2 cloves garlic, minced
- 1 1/2 lbs butternut squash, peeled and cut into bite-size pieces
- 1 (14.5 oz.) can diced tomatoes with chilies
- 1 (14.5 oz.) can vegetable broth
- 1/2 C. water
- 1 tsp ground cumin
- 1 tsp dried oregano
- 1/4 tsp black pepper
- 1 (14.5 oz.) can Green Beans, undrained
- 1 (15 oz.) can black beans, rinsed and drained
- Hot cooked couscous
- Chopped fresh cilantro (optional)

Directions

- Stir fry your garlic and onion for 7 mins in oil. Then add in: black pepper, squash, oregano, diced tomatoes, cumin, water, and broth.
- Get everything boiling for 2 mins, then lower the heat and let the veggies gently boil for 32 mins covered with a lid.
- After 32 mins add both of the beans and cook for 7 more mins.
- Add some cilantro as a garnish.
- Enjoy.

Amount per serving (6 total)

Timing Information:

Preparation	Cooking	Total Time
25 m	35 m	1 h

Nutritional Information:

Calories	262 kcal
Fat	2.2 g
Carbohydrates	52.2g
Protein	10.2 g
Cholesterol	0 mg
Sodium	843 mg

* Percent Daily Values are based on a 2,000 calorie diet.

Couscous XLV

(Tabbouleh I)

Ingredients

- 1 C. low-sodium chicken broth
- 1/2 C. water
- 1 C. couscous
- 1 cucumber, seeded and diced
- 3 green onions, chopped
- 1 carrot, grated
- 1 C. chopped fresh parsley
- 1/4 C. extra-virgin olive oil
- 1/4 C. lemon juice
- 1/4 tsp ground cumin
- 1/2 tsp salt
- 1/2 tsp ground black pepper
- 1/4 C. crumbled feta cheese

Directions

- Boil your couscous in broth and water then place a lid on the pan and shut the heat. Let the contents sit for 12 mins then stir it.
- Get a big bowl, combine: parsley, couscous, carrots, onions, and cucumbers with lemon juice and olive oil.
- Add in some black pepper, cumin, and salt before adding in the cheese.
- Enjoy.

Amount per serving (4 total)

Timing Information:

Preparation	Cooking	Total Time
25 m	5 m	35 m

Nutritional Information:

Calories	309 kcal
Fat	16.6 g
Carbohydrates	33.3g
Protein	7.6 g
Cholesterol	9 mg
Sodium	454 mg

* Percent Daily Values are based on a 2,000 calorie diet.

Couscous XLVI

(Scallops, Parsley, And Parmesan)

Ingredients

- 2 1/2 C. water
- 2 tbsps butter, divided
- 1 tsp salt
- 2 C. pearl (Israeli) couscous
- 1/4 C. extra-virgin olive oil
- 1/4 C. white wine
- 2 tsps grated Parmesan cheese
- 3 cloves garlic, minced
- 1/4 C. chopped fresh parsley
- salt and ground black pepper to taste
- 1 lb bay scallops
- 4 tsps grated Parmesan cheese, or to taste - divided (optional)
- 1 tbsp chopped fresh parsley, or to taste (optional)

Directions

- Boil a tbsp of butter, and salt in water then pour in the couscous and lower the heat.
- Let the couscous gently boil for 12 mins uncovered.
- Stir fry the following spices in butter (1 tbsp) and olive oil for 6 mins to season the butter: parsley, pepper, salt, wine, garlic, parmesan.
- Turn up the heat and add in your scallops and cook for 5 more mins.
- Plate your couscous then add a topping of scallops and also some more parmesan.

- Enjoy.

Amount per serving (4 total)

Timing Information:

Preparation	Cooking	Total Time
15 m	20 m	35 m

Nutritional Information:

Calories	566 kcal
Fat	22.1 g
Carbohydrates	50.4g
Protein	37.1 g
Cholesterol	87 mg
Sodium	1015 mg

* Percent Daily Values are based on a 2,000 calorie diet.

Couscous XLVII

(Lentils, Onions, Feta, And Cranberries)

Ingredients

- 1 C. dried lentils
- 2 bay leaves, divided (optional)
- water to cover
- 2 C. water
- 1 C. couscous

Dressing:
- 3 tbsps lemon juice
- 1 tsp honey
- 1 tbsp white wine vinegar
- 1/4 tsp salt
- 3 tbsps olive oil
- ground black pepper to taste
- 1/2 C. coarsely chopped walnuts, toasted
- 1/2 C. dried cranberries, or to taste
- 1/2 C. crumbled feta cheese
- 1 small green onion, finely chopped

Directions

- Boil your lentils and bay leaf for 32 mins with a low level of heat. Remove any excess liquid.
- Boil your couscous in water, then shut the heat, place a lid on the pot.
- Let the contents sit for 7 mins before stirring it.
- Combine the couscous and lentils.

- Get a bowl, combine: lemon juice, honey, salt, green onions, walnuts, cheese, and cranberries, olive oil, vinegar, and black pepper.
- Top the couscous mix with the lemon juice mix.
- Place everything in the fridge for 30 mins to chill then serve.
- Enjoy.

Amount per serving (12 total)

Timing Information:

Preparation	Cooking	Total Time
15 m	45 m	2 h

Nutritional Information:

Calories	205 kcal
Fat	8.9 g
Carbohydrates	24.7g
Protein	7.8 g
Cholesterol	6 mg
Sodium	123 mg

* Percent Daily Values are based on a 2,000 calorie diet.

Couscous XLVIII

(Pine Nuts And Oranges)

Ingredients

- 1 (10 oz.) box uncooked plain couscous
- 1 (11 oz.) can mandarin oranges, drained and liquid reserved
- 1/4 C. pine nuts, lightly toasted

Directions

- Boil your couscous in the mandarin liquid.
- Then shut the heat, place a lid on the pot, and let the couscous sit for 10 mins until all the liquid has been absorbed, then stir.
- Add in your pine nuts and oranges.
- Enjoy.

Amount per serving (4 total)

Timing Information:

Preparation	Cooking	Total Time
5 m	15 m	20 m

Nutritional Information:

Calories	344 kcal
Fat	4.8 g
Carbohydrates	63.6g
Protein	11.6 g
Cholesterol	0 mg
Sodium	11 mg

* Percent Daily Values are based on a 2,000 calorie diet.

Couscous XLIX

(Buttery Rosemary)

Ingredients

- 1 C. water
- 1/3 C. white cooking wine
- 1 tbsp butter
- 1/2 tsp dried rosemary, crushed
- 1/4 tsp salt
- 1 C. couscous, regular or whole wheat

Directions

- Boil everything except the couscous for 2 mins then pour in the couscous, place a lid on the pot, and let the contents sit for 7 mins with no heat.
- Fluff the couscous with a fork after all the liquid has been absorbed.
- Enjoy.

Amount per serving (4 total)

Timing Information:

Preparation	Cooking	Total Time
15 m		15 m

Nutritional Information:

Calories	202 kcal
Fat	3.2 g
Carbohydrates	33.6g

Protein	5.6 g
Cholesterol	8 mg
Sodium	299 mg

* Percent Daily Values are based on a 2,000 calorie diet.

Couscous L

(Mexican Pineapple And Beans)

Ingredients

- 1/2 C. water
- 1 (15 oz.) can pineapple chunks, drained (juice reserved)
- 1 C. couscous
- 1 (15 oz.) can black beans, rinsed and drained
- 1/3 C. warm water
- 2 tbsps taco seasoning mix

Directions

- Boil .5 C. of water along with the pineapple juice then add in your couscous and place a lid on the pot after shutting the heat.
- Let the couscous sit for 7 mins before stirring it.
- Stir fry the beans and pineapple with taco seasoning and 1/3 C. of water for 8 mins.
- Then top your couscous with the pineapple mix.
- Enjoy.

Amount per serving (2 total)

Timing Information:

Preparation	Cooking	Total Time
10 m	10 m	25 m

Nutritional Information:

Calories	675 kcal

Fat	1.3 g
Carbohydrates	141.2g
Protein	24.7 g
Cholesterol	0 mg
Sodium	1486 mg

* Percent Daily Values are based on a 2,000 calorie diet.

Couscous Li

(Crab, Clams, Bok Choy, And Tomatoes)

Ingredients

- 2 tbsps butter
- 3 tbsps minced garlic
- 2 heads bok choy, chopped
- 1 (15 oz.) can corn, undrained
- 2 (10 oz.) cans baby clams, undrained
- 1 (8 oz.) bottle clam juice
- 1 (14.5 oz.) can diced tomatoes
- 2 C. water
- 1 cube vegetable bouillon
- 1 1/2 C. couscous
- 1 (4.25 oz.) can crabmeat
- 1 C. heavy cream
- 1/4 C. lime juice
- 1 C. red wine
- 2 tsps garlic salt
- 1 tsp ground black pepper

Directions

- Stir fry your bok choy and garlic in butter for 7 mins then add in: couscous, corn, bouillon, clams and juice, water, and tomatoes.
- Set your heat to low and then add in: black pepper, crabmeat, garlic salt, cream, red wine, and lime juice.
- Cook everything for 32 mins uncovered with low heat.
- Enjoy hot.

Amount per serving (6 total)

Timing Information:

Preparation	Cooking	Total Time
15 m	40 m	55 m

Nutritional Information:

Calories	626 kcal
Fat	21.9 g
Carbohydrates	61.8g
Protein	39.5 g
Cholesterol	145 mg
Sodium	1292 mg

* Percent Daily Values are based on a 2,000 calorie diet.

Couscous LII

(Saffron And Harissa)

(Persian Style)

Ingredients

- 2 tbsps warm water
- 5 saffron threads, or more to taste
- 1 C. couscous
- 1 C. vegetable broth
- 1 celery stalk, diced
- 1/4 C. dried currants
- 2 tbsps extra-virgin olive oil
- 1 tbsp lemon juice
- 1 tsp harissa, or to taste
- 1/2 tsp ground cumin
- sea salt to taste

Directions

- Get a bowl, mix: saffron and warm water.
- Boil your couscous in broth then shut the heat after placing a lid on the pot.
- Let the contents stand for 7 mins before stirring the couscous.
- Get a bowl, combine: sea salt, saffron mix, cumin, couscous, celery, harissa, currants, lemon juice, olive oil.
- Place everything in the fridge for 35 mins.
- Enjoy.

Amount per serving (4 total)

Timing Information:

Preparation	Cooking	Total Time
15 m		50 m

Nutritional Information:

Calories	265 kcal
Fat	7.3 g
Carbohydrates	43.2g
Protein	6.3 g
Cholesterol	0 mg
Sodium	228 mg

* Percent Daily Values are based on a 2,000 calorie diet.

Part 2

Introduction

Filling, fast, cheap and healthy, what's not to love about couscous? This delightful side dish is the best compliment to your Holiday meal I guarantee it!

When looking for a weeknight meal, opt for couscous, a quick-cooking grain. Choose any one of these 37 Mouth-Watering Couscous Recipes from around the world for a light and dynamic meal. Easy to make using my simple and easy to follow step by step instructions.

1. Mouth-Watering Mayan Couscous

Yield: Makes 4 Servings

Ingredients:

1 cup couscous
1/2 teaspoon ground cumin
1 teaspoon salt, or to taste
1 1/4 cups boiling water
1 clove unpeeled garlic
1 (15 ounce) can black beans, rinsed and drained
1 cup canned whole kernel corn, drained
1/2 cup finely chopped red onion
1/4 cup chopped fresh cilantro
1 jalapeno pepper, minced
3 tablespoons olive oil
3 tablespoons fresh lime juice, or to taste

To Make:

Step 1. Combine the couscous, cumin, and salt in a large bowl.

Step 2. Stir in the boiling water and seal with plastic wrap.

Step 3. Set aside for 10 minutes.

Step 4. While waiting for the couscous, cook the unpeeled garlic clove in a small skillet over medium-high heat until toasted and the skin has turned golden-brown.

Step 5. Peel the garlic and mince.

Step 6. Stir the garlic into the couscous along with the black beans, corn, onion, cilantro, jalapeno pepper, olive oil, and lime juice.

Step 7. Serve warm or allow to cool.

2. One Of A Kind Savory Couscous

Yield: Makes 4 Servings

Ingredients:

30 g butter
1 onion, finely sliced
1 -2 garlic clove, crushed
1 cup couscous
2 cups chicken stock
2 tablespoons fresh coriander or 2 tablespoons parsley, chopped
salt and pepper

To Make:

Step 1. Heat butter in sauce pan (which has a lid).

Step 2. Add chopped onions, stir and allow to cook until soft.

Step 3. Stir in crushed garlic.

Step 4. Add couscous, stir.

Step 5. Add chicken stock, stir and bring to boil.

Step 6. Remove off heat, cover and allow to stand for 5 minutes.

Step 7. Stir in coriander or parsley.

Step 8. Add salt and pepper to taste.

Step 9. Serve as a side dish.

3. Delectable Spiced Couscous

Yield: Makes 4 Servings

Ingredients:

1/4 cup butter
1/4 teaspoon cinnamon, ground
1/4 teaspoon cardamom, ground
1/8 teaspoon clove, ground
2 1/4 cups chicken stock
1/2 cup currants
1 1/2 cups couscous
2 tablespoons butter
1/2 teaspoon salt
1/4 cup cashews or 1/4 cup pistachios

To Make:

Step 1. Toast and chop cashews or pistachios.

Step 2. Melt 1/4 c butter in medium saucepan over low heat.

Step 3. Add spices and cook 2 minutes, stirring occasionally.

Step 4. Add stock and currants.

Step 5. Can be prepared 4 hours ahead, bring to boil.

Step 6. Mix in couscous and 2 tbsps.
butter.

Step 7. Cover and remove from heat.

Step 8. Let stand 5 minutes.

Step 9. Fluff with fork; season with salt.

Step 10. Transfer couscous to bowl, add nuts and toss well.

4. Fragrant Couscous Royale

Yield: Makes 6 Servings

Ingredients:

1 tablespoon olive oil
2 pounds small chicken thighs
12 ounces Merguez or spicy Italian sausage
1 tablespoon minced garlic
2 onions, minced
2 carrots, peeled and cut into 1/2-inch rounds
1/2 stalk celery, cut into 1/2 inch pieces
1 rutabaga, parsnip, or turnip - peeled and cut into 1-inch cubes
1/2 green bell pepper, cut into 1/4 inch strips
1/2 red bell pepper, cut into 1/4 inch strips
1 (14.5 ounce) can diced tomatoes
1 (15.5 ounce) can garbanzo beans
2 cups chicken stock
2 teaspoons chopped fresh thyme
1 teaspoon turmeric
1 teaspoon cayenne pepper
1/4 teaspoon harissa, or to taste
1 bay leaf
2 zucchini, halved lengthwise and sliced into 1-inch pieces
2 tablespoons extra virgin olive oil
2 cups couscous
2 cups chicken stock
1/2 cup plain yogurt

To Make:

Step 1. Heat olive oil in a large skillet over medium-high heat.

Step 2. Add chicken thighs, skin-side down, and sear until golden brown on both sides; set aside.

Step 3. Reduce heat to medium, add sausage, and cook sausage until no longer pink; set aside.

Step 4. Stir garlic and onions into skillet; cook until onions have softened and turned translucent.

Step 5. Stir in the carrots, celery, rutabaga, green pepper, red pepper, diced tomatoes, garbanzos, and 2 cups chicken stock.

Step 6. Season with thyme, turmeric, cayenne, harissa, and bay leaf.

Step 7. Cut sausage into 1--inch pieces, and add to skillet along with chicken.

Step 8. Cover, and simmer for 30 minutes until chicken is no longer pink.

Step 9. When the chicken is done, stir in the zucchini, and cook until tender, about 5 minutes.

Step 10. While the chicken is cooking, mix 2 tablespoons of extra virgin olive oil (EVOO) into couscous in a heatproof bowl.

Step 11. Bring 2 cups of chicken stock to a boil and stir into the couscous, cover, and keep hot.

Step 12. Serve chicken stew over the couscous with a dollop of yogurt.

5. Luscious Spinach & Onion Couscous

Yield: Makes 7 Servings

Ingredients:

1 medium onion, chopped
2 garlic cloves, minced
2 tablespoons olive oil
1 (14 1/2 ounce) can chicken broth
1 (10 ounce) package frozen chopped spinach
1 (10 ounce) package couscous
3/4 cup fresh grated parmesan cheese
2 tablespoons lemon juice
salt (to taste)
fresh ground pepper (to taste)
1/2 cup chopped pecans, toasted

To Make:

Step 1. In a saucepan, cook and stir onion and garlic in hot oil until tender.

Step 2. Add the broth and spinach; cook and stir frequently until the spinach thaws.

Step 3. Bring mixture to a boil and stir occasionally.

Step 4. Add in couscous; stir to combine.

Step 5. Cover, remove pan from heat, and let stand 5 minutes or until liquid is absorbed.

Step 6. Add remaining ingredients; stir to combine.

Serve immediately.

6. INCREDIBLE SPONTANEOUS COUSCOUS

Yield: Makes 1 Serving

Ingredients:

1 teaspoon olive oil
1 garlic clove, minced
1 cup onion, chopped
1/2 cup frozen corn
1/2 medium tomatoes, chopped
1/4 cup couscous
1/2 cup water
1 teaspoon parsley, chopped
1 teaspoon Tabasco sauce
1/8 teaspoon cayenne

To Make:

Step 1. Sauté the garlic and onions in oil on medium low heat for 10 minutes, or until onions are slightly browned, stirring occasionally.

Step 2. Add corn, tomatoes, couscous and water.

Step 3. Cover and cook on low heat for 5 to 8 minutes, or until all the water is absorbed and the couscous is soft.

Step 4. Add parsley, Tabasco and cayenne.

Step 5. Salt and pepper to taste, if desired.

7. Devil May Care Couscous Primavera

Yield: Makes 6 Servings

Ingredients:

2 cups dry couscous
1/2 cup chopped green onions
1 fresh jalapeno pepper, finely diced
2 tablespoons olive oil
1/2 teaspoon ground cumin
1 pinch cayenne pepper
1 pinch ground black pepper
2 cups vegetable stock
1 bunch asparagus, trimmed and cut into 1/4-inch pieces
1 cup shelled fresh or thawed frozen peas
2 tablespoons chopped fresh mint
salt and freshly ground black pepper to taste

To Make:

Step 1. Combine couscous, green onion, jalapeno, olive oil, cumin, cayenne pepper, and black pepper in a large bowl; stir until olive oil is completely incorporated.

Step 2. Bring vegetable stock, asparagus, and peas to a boil in a saucepan over high heat.

Step 3. Pour stock, asparagus, and peas over couscous mixture; shake bowl to settle couscous into liquid.

Step 4. Cover and let stand for 10 minutes.

Step 5. Fluff with a fork, then stir in mint and season with salt and pepper to taste.

8. Awesome Kittencal's Greek Couscous

Yield: Makes 4 Servings

Ingredients:

1 1/2 cups chicken broth (I use a garlic flavored broth for this) or
1 1/2 cups water (I use a garlic flavored broth for this)
1 cup uncooked couscous
1/2-1 teaspoon dried oregano
2 plum tomatoes, chopped
1 -2 cup diced peeled cucumber
1/2 cup crumbled feta cheese
1/2 cup small ripe olives, halved
1 small red onion, finely chopped
1 (15 ounce) can chickpeas, well drained (garbanzo beans)
1/4 cup water
3 tablespoons lemon juice
2 -3 tablespoons olive oil
1 teaspoon fresh ground black pepper (or to taste)
salt (to taste)

To Make:

Step 1. Bring the 1-1/2 cups chicken broth to a boil in a medium saucepan; stir in the couscous and oregano, remove from heat; cover, and let stand 5 minutes.
Step 2. Fluff with a fork.
Step 3. Combine the couscous with tomatoes and the next 5 ingredients (tomatoes through chickpeas) in a bowl; set aside.
Step 4. Combine 1/4 cup water with the remaining ingredients; stir well with a whisk.
Step 5. Pour over the couscous mixture, tossing gently to coat.

Step 6. Season with black pepper and salt.

9. Dynamic Curried Couscous

Yield: Makes 4 Servings

Ingredients:

2 teaspoons butter
1 (14 1/2 ounce) can reduced-sodium fat-free chicken broth
1/3 cup water
1/2 teaspoon curry powder
1/4 teaspoon ground allspice
1 (10 ounce) package couscous

To Make:

Step 1. Bring the butter, broth, and 1/3 cup water to boil in a medium saucepan.

Step 2. Gradually stir in the curry powder, allspice and couscous.

Step 3. Remove from heat, cover and let stand for 5 minutes.

Step 4. Fluff couscous with a fork.

10. Snappy Cauliflower Couscous

Yield: Makes 6 Servings

Ingredients:

1 head cauliflower, cut into florets
1/4 cup butter
1 small sweet onion (such as Vidalia®), diced
1 clove garlic, minced
9 pitted Kalamata olives
1 teaspoon dried parsley
salt to taste
1 lemon, zested

To Make:

Step 1. Cut cauliflower into very finely chopped pieces similar to real couscous or rice.

Step 2. Melt butter in a medium skillet over medium heat.

Step 3. Add onion and garlic; cook and stir until onion has softened, about 2 minutes.

Step 4. Add cauliflower and cook on medium heat for about 40 minutes.

Step 5. Stir every 5 minutes until entire batch is golden and nutty.

Step 6. Mix Kalamata olives, parsley, salt, and lemon zest into cauliflower.

11. Stimulating Cranberry Couscous Salad

Yield: Makes 6 Servings

Ingredients:

1 1/2 cups chicken broth or 1 1/2 cups vegetable broth
1/2 cup dried cranberries
1 teaspoon ground cinnamon
1/4 teaspoon ground cumin
1 cup uncooked couscous
1/4-1/3 cup vegetable oil
2 tablespoons rice vinegar
1/3-1/2 cup sliced almonds, toasted
1/3 cup chopped green onion
2 tablespoons chopped of fresh mint

To Make:

Step 1. Combine broth, cranberries, cinnamon, and cumin in a medium saucepan.

Step 2. Bring to a boil.

Step 3. Remove broth from heat and stir in couscous.

Step 4. Cover and let stand for 5-7 minutes.

Step 5. Fluff with a fork and set aside to cool slightly, uncovered.

Step 6. Whisk oil and vinegar together; pour over couscous.

Step 7. Add remaining ingredients and toss well.

Step 8. Serve either chilled or at room temperature.

12. Tasty Mediterranean Couscous Salad

Yield: Makes 4 Servings

Ingredients:

1 cup couscous
2 tablespoons lemon juice
2 tablespoons olive oil
1/3 cup green onion
2 medium tomatoes, diced
1 cup canned red kidney beans (only if you want)
1 cup feta cheese
1/4 cup pine nuts
2 tablespoons oregano

To Make:

Step 1. Cook couscous in 1 cup of water.

Step 2. Cool to room temperature.

Step 3. Whisk together lemon juice and olive oil.

Step 4. Pour over other ingredients combining well.

Step 5. Season with fresh pepper.

13. Tempting Black Bean & Couscous Salad

Yield: Makes 8 Servings

Ingredients:

1 cup uncooked couscous
1 1/4 cups chicken broth
3 tablespoons extra virgin olive oil
2 tablespoons fresh lime juice
1 teaspoon red wine vinegar
1/2 teaspoon ground cumin
8 green onions, chopped
1 red bell pepper, seeded and chopped
1/4 cup chopped fresh cilantro
1 cup frozen corn kernels, thawed
2 (15 ounce) cans black beans, drained
salt and pepper to taste

To Make:

Step 1. Bring chicken broth to a boil in a 2 quart or larger sauce pan and stir in the couscous.

Step 2. Cover the pot and remove from heat.

Step 3. Let stand for 5 minutes.

Step 4. In a large bowl, whisk together the olive oil, lime juice, vinegar and cumin.

Step 5. Add green onions, red pepper, cilantro, corn and beans and toss to coat.

Step 6. Fluff the couscous well, breaking up any chunks.

Step 7. Add to the bowl with the vegetables and mix well.

Step 8. Season with salt and pepper to taste and serve at once or refrigerate until ready to serve.

14. Wholesome Spicy Vegetable Couscous

Yield: Makes 4-8 Servings

Ingredients:

1/2 teaspoon vegetable oil
2 green onions, chopped
1 sweet red pepper
1 garlic clove, minced
2 tomatoes, chopped
1 zucchini, diced
1 cup chickpeas, cooked
1 cup boiling water
1/4 teaspoon salt
1/2 teaspoon curry powder
1 teaspoon ground cumin
2 tablespoons fresh parsley
1/8 teaspoon ground cinnamon
1/2 teaspoon ginger
1/4 teaspoon cayenne
1 cup couscous

To Make:

Step 1. In a medium-size skillet heat the oil.

Step 2. Add green onions, sweet pepper, garlic, tomatoes and zucchini; sauté 5 min, stirring.

Step 3. Remove from heat and keep warm.

Step 4. In a medium-size saucepan, combine the remaining ingredients, mix, cover and let stand 5 minutes, until liquid is absorbed.

Step 5. Add the first mixture and fluff with a fork.

15. Relishing Red Bell Pepper Couscous

Yield: Makes 4 Servings

Ingredients:

1 tablespoon olive oil
1 small onion, finely chopped
1/2 red bell peppers or 1/2 green bell pepper, diced
1/4 teaspoon dried thyme
1/4 teaspoon salt
1/4 teaspoon fresh black pepper
1 1/2 cups vegetable broth
1 cup couscous

To Make:

Step 1. In a small saucepan, heat oil at medium heat.

Step 2. Add onion, bell pepper, thyme, salt and pepper and cook, stirring often, for 5 minutes or until veggies have softened.

Step 3. Pour the vegetable broth in the saucepan and bring to boil.

Step 4. Add couscous and stir.

Step 5. Cover and remove from the heat.

Step 6. Let rest 5 minutes.

Step 7. Fluff with a fork.

16. Rich Saffron Couscous

Yield: Makes 4 Servings

Ingredients:

2 tablespoons warm water
5 saffron threads, or more to taste
1 cup couscous
1 cup vegetable broth
1 celery stalk, diced
1/4 cup dried currants
2 tablespoons extra-virgin olive oil
1 tablespoon lemon juice
1 teaspoon harissa, or to taste
1/2 teaspoon ground cumin
 sea salt to taste

To Make:

Step 1. Combine warm water and saffron together in a bowl.

Step 2. Mix couscous and vegetable broth together in a saucepan; bring to a boil.

Step 3. Remove saucepan from heat, cover saucepan, and let sit for 5 minutes.

Step 4. Fluff couscous with a fork and transfer to a bowl.

Step 5. Stir saffron mixture, celery, currants, olive oil, lemon juice, harissa, cumin, and sea salt into couscous.

Step 6. Refrigerate until chilled, at least 30 minutes.

17. AMBROSIAL APRICOT COUSCOUS

Yield: Makes 4 Servings

Ingredients:

1 cup couscous
1 small red onion, small dice
1 1/2 cups low sodium chicken broth, warm
1/4 cup dried apricot, coarsely chopped
1/4 cup whole almond, toasted & coarsely chopped
2 scallions, green parts only
1/4 cup fresh mint leaves, roughly chopped
1/2 bunch fresh cilantro leaves, roughly chopped plus leaves for garnish
1 tablespoon fresh lemon juice
1 pinch lemon zest
1 tablespoon extra-virgin olive oil, plus extra for drizzle
kosher salt & freshly ground black pepper

To Make:

Step 1. In a medium saucepan add 1 TBL extra-virgin olive oil, when it is hot add the red onion, almonds and apricots and sauté gently over low heat until translucent and slightly fragrant.

Step 2. Add the couscous then dump in the warm chicken broth.

Step 3. Stir with a fork to combine.

Step 4. Add lemon zest and cover.

Step 5. Let sit for 10 minutes, then uncover and fluff with a fork again.

Step 6. Coarsely chop the green onions, mint and cilantro; add this to the couscous.

Step 7. Add lemon juice, drizzle with olive oil, and season to taste with salt and pepper.

Step 8. Toss gently to combine.

18. Exquisite Balsamic Chicken With Garlic Couscous

Yield: Makes 4 Servings

Ingredients:

4 chicken breasts
1/3 cup balsamic vinegar
1/2 cup chicken stock
2 tablespoons sugar
1 clove garlic, crushed

For Couscous:
1 1/2 cups couscous
2 1/4 cups boiling chicken stock
2 ounces butter (I use a nondairy margarine)
4 cloves garlic, sliced
2 tablespoons fresh thyme

To Make:

Step 1. Place chicken in a shallow dish and pour over the combined vinegar, chicken stock, sugar and garlic.

Step 2. Let marinate at least 10 minutes per side.

To Make Couscous:

Step 1. pour boiling stock over couscous in a large bowl.

Step 2. Cover tightly with plastic wrap and allow to stand for 5 minutes or until all liquid is absorbed.

Step 3. Heat butter or margarine over medium-low heat and sauté garlic and thyme for about 3 minutes (garlic should be soft but not brown).

Step 4. Add the couscous to the pan and stir for 3 minutes.

To Cook The Chicken:

Step 1. Preheat an oiled frying pan over medium-high heat.

Step 2. Cook chicken about 4 minutes per side.

Step 3. Add the marinade to the pan and cook for an additional 1 minute per side or until the chicken is cooked through and the marinade has thickened.

Step 4. Place couscous and top with chicken and sauce.

19. SAVORY GREEK COUSCOUS

Yield: Makes 3 Servings

Ingredients:

1/4 cup chicken broth
1/2 cup water
1 teaspoon minced garlic
1/2 cup pearl (Israeli) couscous
1/4 cup chopped sun-dried tomatoes
1/4 cup sliced Kalamata olives
2 tablespoons crumbled feta cheese
1 cup canned garbanzo beans, rinsed and drained

1 teaspoon dried oregano
1/2 teaspoon ground black pepper
1 tablespoon white wine vinegar
1 1/2 teaspoons lemon juice

To Make:

Step 1. Pour the chicken broth and water into a saucepan, stir in the garlic, and bring to a boil.

Step 2. Stir in the couscous, cover the pan, and remove from heat.

Step 3. Allow the couscous to stand until all the water has been absorbed, about 5 minutes; fluff with a fork.

Step 4. Allow the couscous to cool to warm temperature.

Step 5. In a large serving bowl, lightly toss the couscous, sun-dried tomatoes, olives, feta cheese, and garbanzo beans.

Step 6. Mix the oregano, black pepper, white wine vinegar, and lemon juice in a small bowl, and pour over the couscous mixture.

Step 7. Toss again to serve.

20. Eye-Opener Moroccan Mushroom Couscous

Yield: Makes 4 Servings

Ingredients:

1/4 cup olive oil

1 lb. fresh mushrooms, sliced
1 small onion, thinly sliced
1 clove garlic
1 teaspoon cumin
1 teaspoon coriander seed, crushed
1/4 teaspoon cinnamon
1/4 teaspoon nutmeg
1/4 teaspoon turmeric
1/4 teaspoon saffron thread
1 1/2 cups orange juice
1 teaspoon lemons, zest of or 1 teaspoon orange zest
1 cup uncooked couscous
1/4 cup raisins
salt & pepper

To Make:

Step 1. Heat 2 tablespoon oil add mushrooms seasoned with salt and pepper sauté till tender.

Step 2. Remove from pan and add 2 tablespoons oil, onions, garlic and spices cook for another 5 minutes.

Step 3. Add orange juice and zest simmering till reduced to 1 cup.

Step 4. In a medium bowl Add 1 cup hot water to couscous and raisins season with salt and pepper remove let stand for 10 minutes.

Step 5. For presentation plate the couscous on a large platter top with mushrooms and pour sauce on top.

Step 6. Just before serving toss together.

21. Scrumptious Fresh Mozzarella, Tomato, & Basil Couscous Salad

Yield: Makes 5 Servings

Ingredients:

2 cups diced tomatoes
3/4 cup diced fresh mozzarella cheese (about 3 ounces)
3 tablespoons minced shallots
2 teaspoons extra virgin olive oil
1/4 teaspoon lemon juice (white balsamic or champagne vinegar okay) or 1/4 teaspoon balsamic vinegar (white balsamic or champagne vinegar okay)
1/2 teaspoon salt, to taste
1/4 teaspoon fresh ground black pepper or 1/4 teaspoon tricolor pepper, to taste
1 garlic clove, crushed and minced
1 1/4 cups water
1 cup uncooked couscous
1/4 cup chopped fresh basil
basil leaves, for garnish (optional)

To Make:

Step 1. In a large bowl combine the tomato, mozzarella, shallots, olive oil, lemon juice, salt, pepper, and garlic, toss well then refrigerate, covered, to marinate for 30 minutes.

Step 2. In a saucepan bring the water to a boil and gradually stir in the couscous; remove from the stove, cover, and set aside for 5 minutes.

Step 3. With a fork, fluff the couscous then let cool.

Step 4. Add the cooled couscous and chopped basil to the tomato mixture in the bowl and toss.

Step 5. Garnish with whole basil leaves and serve.

Note: part-skim mozzarella cheese can be substituted.

22. APPEALING COUSCOUS GOURMET

Yield: Makes 4 Servings

Ingredients:

1 1/4 cups water
1 (10 ounce) box whole wheat couscous with flaxseed
5 teaspoons butter
1 teaspoon chopped fresh basil, or to taste
1 tablespoon olive oil
1 pound fresh asparagus, trimmed and cut into thirds
1 zucchini, sliced
1 red bell pepper, cut into strips
1 clove garlic, minced
salt and ground black pepper to taste
1 sprig fresh basil

To Make:

Step 1. Bring water to a boil in a saucepan and stir in couscous.

Step 2. Bring back to a boil, reduce heat to low, cover the pan, and simmer couscous until water is absorbed, about 5 minutes.

Step 3. Remove from heat and allow to stand covered for about 5 more minutes to let couscous dry.

Step 4. Stir butter and 1 teaspoon basil lightly into couscous until butter is melted; set couscous aside.

Step 5. Heat olive oil in a skillet over medium heat; cook and stir asparagus, zucchini, red bell pepper, and garlic in the hot oil until the vegetables are tender and just starting to brown, about 10 minutes.

Step 6. Season with salt and black pepper.

Step 7. Pack the couscous tightly into a measuring cup or bowl; place serving platter face down on top of the cup, invert the platter, and remove cup to turn couscous out onto the platter in a rounded shape.

Step 8. Arrange cooked vegetables around the mound of couscous; place 1 sprig of basil in center of couscous to serve.

23. DELECTABLE CORN COUSCOUS

Yield: Makes 4 Servings

Ingredients:

1 cup couscous
1/2 teaspoon chicken stock powder
1 cup boiling water
1 tablespoon butter
2 spring onions, chopped
420 g corn, drained
2 tablespoons chopped parsley

To Make:

Step 1. Place the couscous, stock powder and water into a bowl.

Step 2. Cover and allow to stand for 5 mins.

Step 3. Fluff up with a fork.

Step 4. Melt the butter in a pan, add the spring onion and corn, cook 2 minutes.

Step 5. Stir corn into couscous with the parsley and serve.

24. DELICIOUS COUSCOUS TOSS

Yield: Makes 6 Servings

Ingredients:

1 cup no-salt-added chicken broth
1 teaspoon dried basil
1 garlic clove, minced

3/4 cup couscous, uncooked
1 tablespoon white wine vinegar
1 1/2 teaspoons olive oil
1/2 teaspoon black pepper
1/8 teaspoon salt
1 cup tomatoes, seeded and chopped

To Make:

Step 1. Combine chicken broth, basil and garlic in medium saucepan, stirring well; bring to a boil.

Step 2. Remove from heat.

Step 3. Add couscous, cover and let stand 5 minutes.

Step 4. Fluff couscous with a fork.

Step 5. Combine vinegar, olive oil, pepper and salt in a small bowl, stirring with a wire whisk.

Step 6. Add vinegar mixture and tomato to couscous, tossing well.

25. DELISH COUSCOUS CAPRICE

Yield: Makes 4 Servings

Ingredients:

1 cup boiling water
1 cup couscous
4 tomatoes

16 leaves fresh basil
8 ounces fresh mozzarella cheese, diced
1/4 cup balsamic vinegar, or to taste

To Make:

Step 1. Preheat oven to 350 degrees F (175 degrees C).

Step 2. Lightly grease a baking dish.

Step 3. Pour boiling water over couscous in a bowl.

Step 4. Cover bowl with plastic wrap.

Step 5. Let couscous soak until the water is completely absorbed, about 5 minutes.

Step 6. Slice the tops from tomatoes and take a very small slice of the bottoms so they will be stable upright.

Step 7. Use a spoon to remove and discard the tomato innards.

Step 8. Put tomatoes in the prepared baking dish.

Step 9. Bake tomatoes in the preheated oven until lightly charred at the edges, about 20 minutes.

Step 10. Line the inner walls of each tomato with 4 basil leaves.

Step 11. Toss mozzarella cheese with the couscous; stuff into tomatoes.

Step 12. Drizzle balsamic vinegar over the top of the stuffed tomatoes.

26. Divine Baked Couscous With Summer Squash

Yield: Makes 6 Servings

Ingredients:

14 ounces reduced-sodium fat-free chicken broth or 14 ounces vegetable broth, DIVIDED
3/4 cup uncooked couscous
2 cups sliced yellow squash
1/2 cup sliced green onion
2 tablespoons chopped fresh basil
1 tablespoon chopped fresh oregano
1 garlic clove, minced
1/4 cup shredded Fontina cheese
1/4 cup grated parmesan cheese
1/4 cup egg substitute
1/4 teaspoon salt
1/4 teaspoon pepper

To Make:

Step 1. Preheat oven to 400°F.

Step 2. Bring 1 cup of broth to a boil in a medium saucepan; gradually stir in uncooked couscous.

Step 3. Remove from heat; cover and let stand 5 minutes.

Step 4. Fluff couscous with fork.

Step 5. Heat a large nonstick skillet over medium high heat.

Step 6. Coat pan with cooking spray.

Step 7. Add squash, onions, basil, oregano, and garlic; sauté 3 minutes or until squash is tender.

Step 8. Set aside.

Step 9. Combine cheeses; set aside.

Step 10. Combine couscous, squash mixture, and half of cheese mixture in a large bowl; stir in remaining broth, egg substitute, salt, and pepper.

Step 11. Spoon mixture into an 8x8-inch baking dish that is lightly coated with cooking spray.

Step 12. Top with remaining cheese mixture.

Step 13. Bake at 400°F for 25 to 35 minutes or until golden. Mine takes 35.
Serve warm.

27. Heavenly Algerian Couscous

Yield: Makes 3 Servings

Ingredients:

1 large onion, chopped
1/2 teaspoon turmeric
1/4 teaspoon cayenne
1/2 cup vegetable stock
1/2 tablespoon cinnamon

1 1/2 teaspoons black pepper
1/2 teaspoon salt
5 tablespoons tomato puree
3 -4 whole cloves
3 medium zucchini
4 small yellow squash
3/4 large carrot
4 medium yellow potatoes, skins on
1 red bell pepper
1 (15 ounce) can garbanzo beans

To Make:

Step 1. Sauté onion in vegetable stock over med. low heat until translucent.

Step 2. Add all spices and cook for a few more minutes, stirring as needed.

Step 3. Add tomato paste, stir and simmer 2 minutes.

Step 4. Cut the vegetables in large chunks and add all (not the beans) and a dash of cinnamon; add water to cover.

Step 5. Bring to a boil, then reduce heat and simmer, covered, for an hour or so.

Step 6. Add the drained garbanzos about 5 minutes before you take the veggies off the heat.

Step 7. Put couscous in a bowl.

Step 8. Pour boiling water over couscous and wait about 5 minutes.

Step 9. Fluff with fork.

(Ratio of about 1 1/2:1 of water to couscous.).

Step 10. For added flavor, add some of the liquid from the veggie stew to the couscous in place of some of the water.

Step 11. Serve the stew over the couscous.

Enjoy!

28. INVITING LEMON COUSCOUS

Yield: Makes 3 Servings

Ingredients:

1 cup chicken broth
2 tablespoons fresh lemon juice
1 tablespoon lemon zest
1 tablespoon butter
1/4 teaspoon salt
2/3 cup couscous
1 (2 ounce) jar sliced pimento peppers, drained
2 tablespoons toasted pine nuts
2 tablespoons chopped fresh parsley

To Make:

Step 1. Stir chicken broth, lemon juice, lemon zest, butter, and salt together in a saucepan; bring to a boil.

Step 2. Add couscous to the liquid and stir to coat completely.

Step 3. Place a cover on the saucepan, remove from heat, and let couscous soak in hot liquid until the moisture is mostly absorbed, about 5 minutes.

Step 4. Fluff couscous with a fork.

Step 5. Stir pimento peppers, pine nuts, and parsley into the couscous.

29. TANTALIZING ASIAN-STYLE COUSCOUS

Yield: Makes 6 Servings

Ingredients:

vegetable oil or cooking spray
1/2 scallion, sliced
1 1/2 cups water
2 tablespoons soy sauce
1/2 teaspoon sugar
1/4 teaspoon ground ginger
1/4 teaspoon garlic powder
1/8-1/4 teaspoon cayenne pepper
1 cup couscous, uncooked

To Make:

Step 1. Coat bottom of pot with oil or cooking spray.

Step 2. Heat over medium-high flame until hot.

Step 3. Add scallions and sauté until tender.

Step 4. Add water and next five ingredients.

Step 5. Bring to a boil.

Step 6. Remove from heat.

Step 7. Add couscous to pan.

Step 8. Cover and let stand 5 minutes or until liquid is absorbed.

Step 9. Fluff with a fork.

Serve warm.

30. YUMMY BUTTERNUT SQUASH & COUSCOUS

Yield: Makes 5-6 Servings

Ingredients:

For Almonds:
1/4 cup sliced almonds

For Squash:
1 1/2 tablespoons olive oil
2 onions, chopped
2 garlic cloves, minced
1/4 teaspoon cayenne pepper
1/8 teaspoon grated nutmeg
1/8 teaspoon cinnamon
1 cup canned diced tomatoes with juice (from one 15-ounce can)

1 butternut squash, peeled, halved lengthwise, seeded, and cut into 3/4-inch dice (about 2 pounds)
1/4 cup raisins
3 cups vegetable broth or 3 cups chicken broth or 3 cups homemade stock
1 teaspoon salt
1 (14 1/2 ounce) can canned chick-peas, drained and rinsed
3/4 cup chopped fresh parsley, curly or flat leaf

For Couscous:
1 1/2-3 cups water
1 1/2 cups couscous
1/4 teaspoon salt

To Make:

For Almonds:

Step 1. In a small frying pan toast the almonds over moderately low heat, stirring frequently, until golden brown, about 5 minutes.

Step 2. Alternately, you may toast them in a 350 F oven for 5 to 10 minutes.

For Squash:

Step 1. In a Dutch oven or large saucepan, heat the oil over moderately low heat.

Step 2. Add the onions and cook, stirring occasionally, until translucent, about 5 minutes.

Step 3. Add the garlic, cayenne, nutmeg, and cinnamon and cook, stirring, 1 minute longer until fragrant.

Step 4. Stir in the tomatoes, squash, raisins, broth, and 1 teaspoon of the salt and bring to a simmer.

Step 5. Stir in the chickpeas and cook, covered, for 10 minutes.

Step 6. Uncover and simmer until the squash is tender, about 10 minutes more.

Step 7. Stir in the parsley.

For Couscous:

Step 1. Meanwhile, in a medium saucepan, bring the water and 1/4 teaspoon salt to a boil.

Step 2. Follow the directions on your package for the correct amount of water.

(Mine is 2 parts water to 1 part couscous, but this varies)

Step 3. Stir in the couscous.

Step 4. Cover, remove from the heat, and let stand for 5 minutes.

Step 5. Fluff with a fork.

Step 6. Serve the stew over the couscous and top with the toasted almonds.

31. CHOICE MOROCCAN COUSCOUS

Yield: Makes 8 Servings

Ingredients:

1 1/4 teaspoons ground cumin
1/2 teaspoon ground ginger
1/4 teaspoon ground cloves
1/8 teaspoon ground cayenne pepper
1/2 teaspoon ground cardamom
1/4 teaspoon ground coriander
1/4 teaspoon ground allspice
1 tablespoon olive oil
1 red onion, cut in half and thinly sliced
1 red, green, or yellow bell pepper, cut into 1" pieces
2 zucchinis, halved lengthwise and cut into 3/4 inch pieces
1/2 cup golden raisins
1 teaspoon kosher salt
grated zest of one orange
1 (14.5 ounce) can low sodium garbanzo beans, rinsed and drained
1 1/2 cups chicken broth
1/2 cup orange juice
1 1/2 cups couscous
3 tablespoons chopped fresh mint

To Make:

Step 1. Place a large, heavy bottomed pot over medium heat.

Step 2. Stir in the cumin, ginger, cloves, cayenne, cardamom, coriander, and allspice; gently toast until fragrant, about 2 to 3 minutes.

Step 3. Stir in oil and onion, cook until softened.

Step 4. Stir in the bell pepper, and zucchini; cook for 5 minutes.

Step 5. Stir in the raisins, salt, zest, and garbanzos.

Step 6. Pour in the chicken broth and orange juice; turn heat to high and bring to a boil.

Step 7. When the mixture is boiling, stir in the couscous and remove from heat; cover, and let stand 5 minutes.

Step 8. Fluff with a fork, and fold in chopped mint.

32. Tasteful Mandarin Couscous Salad

Yield: Makes 7 Servings

Ingredients:

1 1/3 cups water
1 cup couscous, uncooked
1 (11 ounce) can mandarin oranges, drained
1 cup frozen peas, thawed
1/2 cup slivered almonds, toasted
1/3 cup red onion, chopped (I'd probably use Vidalia)
3 tablespoons cider vinegar or 3 tablespoons white vinegar
2 tablespoons olive oil
1 tablespoon sugar
1/4 teaspoon salt
1/4 teaspoon hot pepper sauce

To Make:

Step 1. Place water in a saucepan and bring to a boil.

Step 2. Stir in couscous and cover then remove from heat and let stand for 5 minutes.

Step 3. Fluff with a fork then recover and refrigerate for at least one hour.

Step 4. In a bowl, combine the oranges, peas, almonds, onion and couscous.

Step 5. In a jar with a tight lid, combine the vinegar, oil, sugar, salt and hot pepper sauce then shake well.

Step 6. Pour dressing over couscous mixture and toss to coat.

33. Ambrosia Golden Couscous

Yield: Makes 8 Servings

Ingredients:

3 tablespoons butter
3 tablespoons olive oil or 3 tablespoons vegetable oil
3 medium onions, finely chopped (or use 2 large onion)
1 teaspoon brown sugar
1 tablespoon fresh minced garlic (optional)
1 pinch cayenne pepper
3 teaspoons turmeric
2 teaspoons cumin
1-2 teaspoon fresh ground black pepper
3 cups couscous
6 cups hot low sodium chicken broth
3/4 cup currants

1/2 cup slivered almonds
seasoning salt (to taste) or white salt (to taste)

To Make:

Step 1. Bring the broth to a boil; cover with a lid to keep hot; set aside.

Step 2. In a large skillet melt the butter with oil over medium-high heat.

Step 3. Add in chopped onions with 1 teaspoon brown sugar; sauté stirring until light golden brown (about 15 minutes).

Step 4. Add in the garlic, cayenne, turmeric, cumin and ground black pepper; stir for 2 minutes.

Step 5. Add in couscous and stir until coated with the onion mixture.

Step 6. Mix in the hot broth and currants; cover with a lid.

Step 7. Remove from heat and let stand for about 10-15 minutes or until all the water is absorbed.

Step 8. Fluff with a fork then mix in the almonds, then season with salt and more ground black pepper if desired.

34. Tempting Israeli Couscous & Cheese

Yield: Makes 4 Servings

Ingredients:

2 teaspoons butter
1 cup pearl (Israeli) couscous
2 cups chicken broth
1/2 cup heavy cream
1/4 cup diced pimientos
1 pinch cayenne pepper, or more to taste
3 ounces shredded sharp Cheddar cheese
1 tablespoon chopped fresh chives
salt and freshly ground black pepper to taste

To Make:

Step 1. Melt butter in a large skillet over medium heat.

Step 2. Cook and stir couscous in the melted butter until slightly toasted, 2 to 3 minutes.

Step 3. Pour in chicken broth and bring to a boil. Reduce heat to low and simmer until most of the stock is absorbed and the couscous have plumped, 6 to 7 minutes.

Step 4. Stir heavy cream and pimientos into couscous; add cayenne pepper and cook until couscous is tender, 2 to 3 minutes.

Step 5. Add more broth if needed.

Step 6. Remove from heat and stir in Cheddar cheese until melted; add chives and stir to combine.

Step 7. Season with salt, black pepper, and cayenne pepper to taste.

35. Titillating Lentil & Couscous Salad

Yield: Makes 8 Servings

Ingredients:

1/2 cup red onion, chopped finely
1/4 cup lemon juice
2 tablespoons red wine vinegar
1 cup lentils
5 cups water
1/3 cup extra virgin olive oil, plus
1 tablespoon extra-virgin olive oil
1 cup couscous
4 tablespoons fresh parsley, chopped
4 tablespoons of fresh mint, chopped
3 scallions, white and light green part only, sliced thin
salt and pepper

To Make:

Step 1. Combine red onion, lemon juice and vinegar in large bowl with a pinch of salt.

Step 2. Put lentils and 4 cups of water in pot and bring to boil then simmer for 20 minutes or til lentils are soft.

Step 3. Take off heat and let rest for 5 minutes.

Step 4. Drain and add to onion mixture along with the 1/3 cup of olive oil.

Step 5. Toss well.

Step 6. Bring 1 cup of water to boil, add couscous, take off heat, cover and let stand for 5 minutes.

Step 7. Fluff up the couscous by raking with a fork and adding slowly the 1 T of olive oil.

Step 8. Try to get rid of the clumps.

Step 9. Add the couscous to the lentil mixture along with the parsley, mint and scallions.

Step 10. Salt and pepper to taste.

36. A SHOCKER COUSCOUS WITH A KICK

Yield: Makes 6 Servings

Ingredients:

3 cups water
2 cups couscous
1/2 cup crumbled feta cheese
1 fresh jalapeno pepper, chopped
1/2 cucumber, diced
1 clove garlic, minced
1/2 cup chopped green onion
3 tablespoons chopped fresh mint
3 tablespoons chopped fresh basil
3 tablespoons chopped fresh cilantro
1 tablespoon chopped fresh parsley

2 teaspoons ground cumin
2 teaspoons cayenne pepper
1 lemon, juiced

To Make:

Step 1. Bring the water to a boil in a saucepan.

Step 2. Remove from the heat and stir in the couscous.

Step 3. Cover and let stand until the couscous absorbs the water entirely, about 10 minutes; fluff with a fork.

Step 4. While the couscous soaks, stir the feta cheese, jalapeno pepper, cucumber, garlic, green onion, mint, basil, cilantro, parsley, cumin, cayenne pepper, and lemon juice in a large bowl.

Step 5. Add the prepared couscous and mix well.

37. GOTTA HAVE IT JEWELED COUSCOUS

Yield: Makes 4 Servings

Ingredients:

3 cups vegetable stock
12 ounces uncooked couscous
1 lemon, grated rind only
4 tablespoons extra virgin olive oil
2 ounces toasted sliced almonds
3 ounces dried apricots, chopped
2 ounces sultanas or 2 ounces golden raisins

3 tablespoons chopped fresh parsley
salt & freshly ground black pepper

To Make:

Step 1. Boil stock in a saucepan.

Step 2. Pour in the couscous in a thin stream and stir in lemon rind.

Step 3. Cover the pan, remove from heat and leave for 5 minutes, fluffing with a fork after 2 minutes.

Step 4. Drizzle over olive oil and stir in almonds, apricots, sultanas and parsley.

Step 5. Season.

Step 6. Either serve immediately or cover with foil and keep warm in the oven for up to 30 minutes, or allow to cool, cover with plastic wrap and reheat in a microwave oven.

Pesto And Feta Couscous Fritters

Makes 6-8 small fritters
Prep Time: 7 minutes   Cook Time: 7-10 minutes
1 cup/240ml - Vegetable Broth
1 cup/175g - Moroccan Couscous
1 egg, slightly beaten
2 Tbsp - Basil Pesto
3 oz/85g - Feta Cheese
4 green onions (spring onions), chopped
2 Tbsp - Olive Oil,

1. In a medium saucepan, bring the vegetable broth to a boil. Add the couscous, cover with lid, and immediately remove from heat.
2. Allow the couscous to steam (covered) for about 5 minutes or until all liquid is absorbed.
3. Let the couscous cool slightly and then add both the egg and pesto. Mix well.
4. Gently stir in the feta cheese and green onions. Set aside.
5. In a large skillet, heat the olive oil over medium heat. Meanwhile, shape the couscous mixture into individual patties. Each patty will use approximately ¼ cup of the

couscous mixture. (Slightly wet your hands before shaping the patties to prevent it sticking to your hands)
6. Cook the patties for 3 minutes on each side or until golden brown.

Couscous Stuffed Tomatoes

Serves 4
Prep Time: 7 minutes   Cook Time: 30 minutes
4 Tomatoes
1 ½ cups/360g - Moroccan Couscous
1 ½ cups/360ml - Vegetable broth
1/4 tsp - Garlic powder
1/4 tsp - Black Pepper
2 ½ Tbsp/35g - Parmesan Cheese
Drizzle of Olive Oil

1. Preheat oven to 375° Fahrenheit.
2. In a medium saucepan, bring 1 ½ cups of vegetable broth to a boil. Add the dry couscous, stir, cover the saucepan and remove from heat.
3. Allow the couscous to steam for approximately 5 minutes or until all the liquid has been absorbed. Set aside and allow to cool slightly.

4. Gently wash the tomatoes and dry with a paper towel. Cut off the "cap" of each tomato and remove the insides with a spoon. If needed, use a little bit of water to rinse out the inside of the tomatoes. Use a paper towel to dry each tomato completely and set aside.
5. To the cooled couscous, add the garlic powder, salt, pepper, and parmesan cheese. Mix well.
6. Spoon the couscous mixture into the tomato shells and drizzle with olive oil. Bake the Tomatoes in a glass baking dish for 25 minutes. Serve warm and enjoy!

TOASTED ALMOND ISRAELI COUSCOUS

Serves 4
Prep Time: 15 minutes   Cook Time: 18-20 minutes
3 Tbsp - butter (divided)
Drizzle of Olive Oil
½ cup/50g - slivered almonds
1 onion, chopped
1 ½ cup/260g - Israeli couscous
½ Tsp - cinnamon
1 bay leaf

1 ¾ cup/420ml - vegetable broth
4 Tbsp - parsley, finely chopped salt and pepper to taste

1. In a medium saucepan, heat 1 Tbsp of butter and a drizzle of oil over medium heat. Add the almonds and toast until golden. Remove almonds from heat with a slotted spoon and set aside.
2. In that same saucepan, add the onion, couscous, bay leaf, and cinnamon and sauté until the onions are transparent and the couscous is slightly browned.
3. Add the vegetable broth to the pan and bring to a boil. Reduce heat to low and cover the couscous. Allow the couscous to steam until all the liquid is absorbed.
4. Remove the couscous from the heat and gently stir in the toasted almonds and parsley. Add salt and pepper to taste.

SOUTH OF THE BORDER DIP

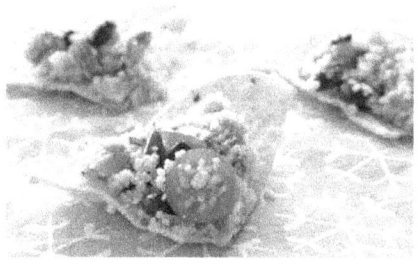

Serves 4-6
Prep Time: 8 minutes   Cook Time: 5 minutes
1 cup/175g - Moroccan couscous
1 cup/240ml - chicken broth
1 small tomato, diced
½ a red onion, diced

1 avocado, cut into bite-sized pieces
1 400g can, black beans (drained)
4 Tbsp fresh cilantro, chopped
For the Dressing
6 Tbsp. extra virgin olive oil
4 Tbsp. fresh lime juice (1 lime)
2 Tsp. red wine vinegar
1 Tsp. ground cumin

1. In a medium saucepan, bring broth to a boil. Add the dry couscous, stir, cover the saucepan and remove from heat.
2. Allow the couscous to steam for approximately 5 minutes or until all the liquid has been absorbed. Gently fluff the couscous with a fork and transfer to a serving bowl.
3. Add the diced tomatoes, red onions, avocado, black beans, and cilantro to the couscous and stir.
4. Finally, whisk the olive oil, vinegar, lime juice, and cumin together in a separate bowl to create the spicy dressing. Drizzle the dressing over the couscous mixture and give it a quick stir.
5. Serve with tortilla chips.

Couscous 'N' Cheese

Serves 2

Prep Time: 5 minutes   Cook Time: 15 minutes
1 Tbsp - olive oil
1 cup/175g - Israeli couscous
1 ¾ cup/420ml - chicken broth ¼ cup/35g - goat cheese
2 Tbsp - sour cream
½ cup/60g - shredded cheddar cheese
salt and pepper, to taste
½ cup/70g - shredded chicken (optional)
sprig of parsley to garnish (optional)

1. In a medium saucepan, heat the olive oil over medium heat and add the couscous. Stir the couscous in the olive oil until slightly browned. Add the chicken stock and bring to a boil. Reduce the heat to low, cover, and cook the couscous until all the liquid is absorbed (about 10 minutes).
2. While the couscous is still hot, add the goat cheese, sour cream, and cheddar cheese. Stir well to incorporate the cheeses (if the couscous isn't creamy enough for your taste, feel free to add additional sour cream)
3. Finally, season the couscous with salt and pepper and add the chicken and parsley if desired.

MEDITERRANEAN SALAD

Serves 2

Prep Time: 20 minutes   Cook Time: 10 mintues
1 cup/240ml - vegetable broth
3/4 cup/130g - Israeli couscous
8 - sliced grape or plum tomatoes
1 cup/100g - sliced and peeled cucumber
½ cup/60g - pitted kalamata olives
2 Tbsp/20g - crumbled feta cheese
4 Tbsp -chopped parsley
2 Tbsp - lemon juice
2 Tbsp - olive or vegetable oil
1/8 Tsp - salt

1. In a medium saucepan, bring the vegetable broth to a boil. Add the dry Israeli couscous, stir, and cover. Reduce the heat to low and cook for about 5 minutes.
2. Remove from heat and allow the couscous to steam until all the liquid has been absorbed.
3. Allow the couscous to cool slightly and then add the vegetables and cheese. Gently stir in the vegetables and set aside.
4. In a small bowl, combine the lemon juice, olive oil, salt and pepper. Whisk until the oil and lemon juice are no longer separated. Drizzle the dressing on the couscous mixture and toss to coat.

Couscous Cleanse

Serves 3

Prep Time: 7-10 minutes   Cook Time: 20 minutes

4 Tbsp - extra-virgin olive oil, divided
2 Tbsp - lemon juice
2 large garlic cloves, finely minced, divided
½ Tsp - finely grated lemon peel
1 ½ cups/260g - Israeli couscous
2 cups/480ml - vegetable broth
2 cups/270g - trimmed asparagus spears, 1-inch pieces
1 ½ cups/190g - snap peas, trimmed, cut into ½-inch pieces
2 Tsp - lemon zest
½ cup/50g - finely grated Parmesan cheese

1. In a small bowl, whisk 2 tablespoons oil, lemon juice, minced garlic, and lemon peel in small bowl; set dressing aside.
2. In a medium saucepan heat 1 Tbsp of oil over medium heat. Add couscous, sprinkle with salt, and sauté until most of couscous is golden brown, about 5 minutes.
3. Add broth, increase heat, and bring to boil. Reduce heat to low, cover, and simmer until liquid is absorbed (about 10 minutes)
4. While the couscous is steaming, heat remaining 1 tablespoon oil in a large skillet over medium high heat. Add asparagus, snap peas, green peas and garlic.
5. Sprinkle with salt and pepper; sauté until tender (about 3 minutes). Transfer vegetables to large bowl.
6. Add couscous to bowl with vegetables and drizzle on dressing. Add Parmesan cheese and lemon zest and toss to coat.

No Cream Broccoli Cheese Soup

Serves 2
Prep Time: 5 minutes   Cook Time: 30 minutes
3 cups/270g - broccoli florets
3 cups/700ml - water
1 cup/175g - Lebanese couscous
1 cup/240ml - vegetable broth
¼ cup/25g - parmesan cheese, shredded
¼ Tsp - salt
¼ Tsp - freshly ground black pepper

1. In a large pot, combine the water, broccoli and couscous. Bring to a boil, reduce heat then simmer uncovered for 25 minutes or until the broccoli is soft and the couscous is tender.
2. With a slotted spoon, scoop the broccoli and couscous into a blender. Add the one cup of vegetable broth and puree until smooth. (The warm broccoli and couscous will expand in the blender so blend small amounts at a time if you have a small blender)
3. Finally add the parmesan, salt and pepper and blend well.
4. Return to stove and simmer for 5 more minutes. Serve with grated Parmesan cheese.

Caramelised Onion And Mushroom Quiche With Couscous Crust

Serves 6
Prep Time: 10 minutes Cook   Time: 60 minutes
½ cup/90g - Moroccan couscous
½ cup/120ml - vegetable stock
1 Tbsp - butter
2 thinly sliced onions
1 Tbsp - olive oil
3 eggs
2 Tbsp - plain greek yogurtv
½ cup/70g - crumbled goat cheese
½ cup/60g - cheddar cheese
¼ cup/25g - Parmesan Cheese
½ cup/50g - sliced mushrooms
4 Tbsp - chopped basil

1. Preheat oven to 375° Fahrenheit and lightly grease a 8 inch tart pan with removable bottom. Set aside.
2. In a medium saucepan, bring vegetable broth to a boil. Add the dry couscous, stir, cover the saucepan and remove from heat.
3. Allow the couscous to steam for approximately 5 minutes or until all the liquid has been absorbed. Set aside and allow to cool slightly.

4. Pour the couscous into the tart pan and press an even layer across the bottom and up the sides of the pan. Wet your fingers to avoid the couscous from sticking to your hands.
5. Bake the crust for 15 minutes. Meanwhile, sauté the mushrooms and onions in olive oil over medium-high heat until tender. Remove from heat and set aside.
6. In a medium bowl, combine the eggs, yogurt, salt, and pepper. Mix well with a fork.
7. To assemble the quiche, pour the vegetables into the bottom of the crust. Next, layer with parmesan cheese, cheddar cheese and crumbled goat cheese. Finally, pour the egg mixture on top and sprinkle with the chopped basil.
8. Bake the Quiche for 40 minutes at 375° Fahrenheit. This should ensure that the egg is cooked all the way through.

CAPRESE COUSCOUS SALAD

Serves 2
Prep Time: 5 minutes   Cook Time: 10 minutes
1 Tbsp - olive oil
 1 cup/175g - Israeli couscous
 1 ½ cup/360ml - vegetable broth
 ¾ cup/130g - cherry tomatoes, sliced

½ cup/60g - fresh mozzarella, cubed
4 Tbsp - fresh basil, chopped
For the Dressing
2 Tbsp - Balsamic Vinegar
2 Tsp - olive oil
salt and pepper, to taste

1. In a medium saucepan, sauté the Israeli couscous in 1 Tbsp olive oil until it just begins to brown. Add the vegetable broth and bring to a boil. Reduce the heat to low and cook for about 5 minutes.
2. Remove from heat and allow the couscous to steam until all the liquid has been absorbed.
3. Allow the couscous to cool slightly and then add the vegetables and cheese. Gently stir in the vegetables and set aside.
4. In a small bowl, combine the balsamic vinegar, olive oil, salt and pepper. Whisk until the oil and vinegar are no longer separated. Drizzle the dressing on the couscous mixture and toss to coat.

CHICKEN AND ZUCCHINI COUSCOUS SAUTÉ

Serves 2
Prep Time: 7 minutes   Cook Time: 20 minutes
2 chicken breasts
3 large zucchini (courgette)
1 cup/175g - Moroccan Couscous
2 Tbsp - olive oil, divided
½ Tsp - ground cumin
salt and pepper, to taste
1 cup/250ml - boiling water
2 Tbsp - fresh parsley, chopped

1. In a skillet, heat oil over medium-high heat. Place chicken breasts in the hot oil and cook for 4-5 minutes per side until cooked through.
2. Cut zucchini into 1/4-inch sticks. In a second skillet, cook zucchini in oil with cumin and salt and pepper to taste over moderate heat until tender, about 5 minutes.
3. Add water and bring to a boil. Stir in couscous and remove skillet from heat.
4. Let mixture stand, covered, 5 minutes. Fluff couscous with a fork and sprinkle with fresh parsley. Top with warm chicken and zucchini.

ROASTED BUTTERNUT SQUASH WITH ISRAELI COUSCOUS

Serves 3

Prep Time: 10 minutes   Cook Time: 30 minutes

1 lemon
1 ½ pound/700g - butternut squash, peeled and seeded, and cut into ¼-inch cubes
3 Tbsp - olive oil
1 large onion, chopped
1 ¾ cups/300g - Israeli couscous
1 cinnamon stick
½ cup/50g - almonds, toasted
½ cup/75g - golden raisins
¼ Tsp - ground cinnamon
8 Tbsp - fresh flat-leaf parsley, chopped

1. Preheat oven to 475°F.
2. Toss squash with 1 tablespoon oil and salt to taste in a large baking pan and spread in 1 layer. Roast in oven 15 minutes, or until squash is just tender, and transfer to a large bowl.
3. Cook onion in 1 tablespoon oil in a large skillet over moderately high heat until translucent. Add to squash.
4. Cook couscous with cinnamon stick in a large pot of boiling salted water 13 minutes and drain in a colander (do not rinse). Add couscous to vegetables and toss with 2 tablespoon olive oil to coat.
5. Add lemon zest, parsley, nuts, raisins, ground cinnamon, and salt to taste. Toss to mix well.

Spicy Fish And Sausage Soup

Serves 2
Prep Time: 7 minutes   Cook Time: 27-30 minutes
2 large Italian Sausages
¼ onion, diced
1 clove garlic, minced
2 large tomatoes, diced
1 ½ cups/360ml - vegetable broth
½ cup/125ml - water
¼ cup/50g - Lebanese Couscous
2 tilapia fillets
½ Tsp - chilli powder
½ Tsp - dried basil
½ Tsp - salt or more to taste
¼ Tsp - pepper or more to taste
1 Tbsp - Fresh Basil
Lemon zest to garnish

1. In a large skillet, cook the sausages over medium high heat until browned on the outside and no longer pink on the inside. Remove the sausages from the pan, but reserve the drippings.

2. To the sausage drippings add the onion and garlic and sauté for 3 minutes. Add the tomatoes and cook for another 3-5 minutes. Add the vegetable stock and water and bring to a boil.
3. Cook for 2 minutes and then add the couscous. Turn down the heat to a simmer and add the fish filets, chilli powder, dried basil, salt, and pepper. Cover and cook until fish and couscous is done (5-7 minutes)
4. Divide between 2 dishes, breaking the fish into large pieces. Garnish with lemon zest and fresh basil.

Roasted Moroccan Couscous With Eggplant

Serves 4
Prep Time: 10 minutes   Cook Time: 55 minutes
4 small eggplant (aubergine)
 2-3 Tbsp - olive oil
 1 medium onion, finely chopped
 ¾ cup/130g - Moroccan couscous
 1 Tbsp - freshly grated lemon zest

¼ cup/40g - feta cheese
½ Tsp - garlic powder
1 Tsp - salt
½ Tsp - freshly ground black pepper
4 Tbsp - roughly chopped fresh flat-leaf parsley, plus more for garnish

1. Preheat oven to 400° degrees.
2. Cut 4 eggplant in half lengthwise, and place the 8 halves cut side up. Using a small knife, cut around the perimeter or each eggplant, leaving a 1/3-inch-wide border and being careful not to cut through skin.
3. Cutting down through flesh, cut lengthwise into 1/4-inch-wide strips. Use a spoon to scoop out the strips, keeping skin intact. Cut strips into 1/4-inch dice. Set both the diced eggplant and shells aside.
4. In a large skillet warm 2 tablespoons olive oil over medium heat. Add onion, and cook, stirring occasionally, until soft and golden (approximately 5 minutes)
5. Add 1/2 teaspoon salt, 1/4 teaspoon black pepper, and ½ teaspoon garlic powder. Cook until browned, 6 to 8 minutes. If mixture starts to become dry, add extra olive oil. Set aside.
6. Meanwhile, bring 1 cup of water to a boil. Add the dry couscous and remove from heat. Cover and allow the couscous to steam (approximately 5 minutes). Fluff with couscous with a fork.
7. Add lemon zest, feta, parsley, remaining 1/2 teaspoon salt, and remaining 1/4 teaspoon pepper to the couscous. Add the reserved eggplant mixture. Stir to combine.
8. Fill each reserved eggplant shell with couscous mixture. Cover with aluminium foil. Bake until warm throughout and shell has softened, 20 to 25 minutes. Remove foil, and continue cooking until tops are golden (about 20 minutes).
9. Remove from oven. Sprinkle with extra parsley (if desired), and serve warm.

Chicken And Mini-Dumplings

Serves 4
Prep Time: 10 minutes   Cook Time: 55 - 60 minutes
2 chicken breasts, cubed into bite-sized pieces
1 cup/175g - Lebanese couscous
¼ onion, chopped
2 large carrots, chopped
¾ cup/75g - mushrooms, sliced
½ cup/45g - broccoli florets, chopped
1 can cream of chicken soup
2 cans of water
1 bay leaf
½ Tsp - chilli powder
¼ Tsp - cumin

1. In a large soup pot, sauté onion and chicken breast in olive oil over medium high heat for 5 minutes or until onion is translucent. Add the vegetables, cream of chicken soup, and water and bring to a boil.
2. Add the Lebanese couscous and seasonings. Give the mixture a few stirs and reduce heat to low. Simmer for 45 minutes to 1 hour, covered. The chicken should be cooked through and the couscous tender.

Lemon Salmon With Green Onion Couscous

Serves 2
Prep Time: 5 minutes   Cook Time: 20 minutes
2 salmon fillets
2 Tbsp - olive oil, divided
1 cup/175g - Moroccan couscous
1 cup/240ml - vegetable broth
4 green onions (spring onions), chopped
1 lemon, both zest and juice will be used.
½ Tsp - salt, divided
½ Tsp - pepper, divided

1. Preheat oven to 350 ° Fahrenheit. Lightly oil a baking sheet and set aside.
2. Season salmon fillets with lemon zest, black pepper, and salt. Place in the baking dish and drizzle lightly with olive oil.
3. Bake the salmon for 15 minutes or until fillet gently flakes apart with a fork
4. Meanwhile, bring vegetable broth and lemon juice to a boil in medium saucepan. Add the couscous, stir, cover, and remove from heat. Allow the couscous to steam for approximately 5 minutes or until all the liquid has been absorbed.

5. Place the salmon filet over a bed of couscous and sprinkle with freshly chopped green onions. Squeeze extra lemon juice on the dish if desired.

RHUBARB COUSCOUS CRISP

Serves 6-8
Prep Time: 10 minutes   Cook Time: 30-35 minutes
5 cups fresh rhubarb, chopped
¾ cup/128g - brown sugar
½ cup/70g - rolled oats
½ cup/85g - brown sugarv ¼ cup+3 Tbsp/55g - flour
¼ Tsp - cinnamon
¼ cup/2oz - butter

1. Preheat oven to 375° Fahrenheit and lightly butter a 2 quart baking dish.
2. Place the chopped rhubarb in the baking dish and mix with the ¾ cup brown sugar until rhubarb is well coated. Set aside.
3. In a mixing bowl, prepare the topping. Combine the oats, ½ cup brown sugar, flour, and cinnamon. Mix well. Cut the butter into the flour mixture using a pastry blender. The mixture should resemble crumbs (approximately the size of peas).
4. Sprinkle the topping evenly over the rhubarb. Bake for 30 to 35 minutes or until the topping is golden brown.

Chocolate And Coconut Couscous Bars

Makes 12 bars
Prep Time: 10 minutes   Cook Time: 40 minutes
1 Tsp - Vanilla
1 Egg
¼ cup/56ml - Vegetable Oil
¼ cup/56ml - Water
1 cup/225ml - Frozen Apple Juice Concentrate
Pinch of Sea Salt
2 Tsp - Baking Powder
2 cups/350g - Moroccan couscous (cooked in water)
1 cup/120g - Whole Wheat Flour
1 ¼ cup/175g - Rolled Oats
Topping
¼ cup/25g - Coconut Flakes
½ Tsp - ground Nutmeg
1 Tsp - ground Cinnamon
¼ cup/25g - slivered almonds
¼ cup/56ml - Frozen Apple Juice Concentrate

1. Preheat oven to 350°F. Lightly butter a 9" x 13" baking pan; set aside.
2. In a large mixing bowl, mix together the flour, baking powder, salt and oats.

3. In a separate bowl, mix together the apple juice concentrate, water, egg and vanilla.
4. Combine the wet ingredients with the dry mixture. Finally, add the couscous to mixture and gently stir. Pour batter into prepared baking pan.
5. For the topping, combine all ingredients in a small bowl; blend well and spread over the batter.
6. Bake for 40 minutes. Cool and cut into squares.

Honey Cinnamon Couscous Pudding

Serves 4
Prep Time: 3 minutes   Cook Time: 15 minutes
1 cup/175g - Moroccan couscous
3 cups/675ml - low-fat milk
¼ cup/88g - honey
1 Tsp - cinnamon
1 Tsp - freshly grated orange zest
1 Tsp - vanilla extract
Ground cinnamon for dusting pudding

1. Heat milk, honey, and cinnamon in a saucepan over mediumhigh heat until nearly simmering.

2. Stir in couscous and vanilla, remove from the heat and cover. Let stand until most of the milk has been absorbed (about 15 minutes)
3. To serve, spoon into bowls and sprinkle with ground cinnamon. Serve warm.

WATERMELON AND FETA COUSCOUS PARFAIT

Serves 2
Prep Time: 7-10 minutes   Cook Time: 10-13 minutes
¾ cup/130g - Israeli couscous
1 cup/225ml - water
1 Tsp - sugar
1 Tsp - vanilla
½ Tsp - lemon juice
1 cup - watermelon, small cubes
¼ cup/40g - feta cheese
½ Tsp - lemon zest
2 sprigs mint

1. In a medium saucepan, bring water, sugar, vanilla, and lemon juice to a boil. (Stir the sugar until it dissolves).

2. Add the Israeli couscous, cover, and remove from heat. Allow the couscous to steam until all the water is absorbed (approximately 10-13 minutes). Fluff the couscous with a fork and allow to cool. This dish is best served chilled.
3. When the couscous has chilled, gently stir in the watermelon cubes and feta cheese. Spoon the mixture into bowls or glasses and garnish with lemon zest and mint sprigs.

www.ingramcontent.com/pod-product-compliance
Lightning Source LLC
Chambersburg PA
CBHW071436070526
44578CB00001B/102